ITALY

ITALY

By the Editors of Time-Life Books
With photographs by Romano Cagnoni

TIME-LIFE BOOKS · AMSTERDAM

TIME-LIFE BOOKS INC.

EDITOR: George Constable
Executive Editor: George Daniels
Editorial General Manager: Neal Goff
Director of Design: Louis Klein
Director of Editorial Resources: Phyllis K. Wise
Editorial Board: Dale M. Brown, Roberta Conlan, Ellen
Phillips, Donia Ann Steele, Rosalind Stubenberg,
Kit van Tulleken, Henry Woodhead
Director of Research and Photography: John
Conrad Weiser

PRESIDENT: Reginald K. Brack Jr.
Executive Vice Presidents: John M. Fahey Jr.,
Christopher T. Linen
Senior Vice President: James L. Mercer
Vice Presidents: Stephen L. Bair, Edward Brash, Ralph J.
Cuomo, Juanita T. James, Wilhelm R. Saake, Robert H.
Smith, Paul R. Stewart, Leopoldo Toralballa

Editorial Operations
Copy Chief: Diane Ullius
Editorial Operations: Caroline A. Boubin (manager)
Production: Celia Beattie
Quality Control: James J. Cox (director)
Library: Louise D. Forstall

LIBRARY OF NATIONS

This book was created in London for
Time-Life Books B.V.

EUROPEAN EDITOR: Kit van Tulleken
Assistant European Editor: Gillian Moore
Design Director: Ed Skyner
Photography Director: Pamela Marke
Chief of Research: Vanessa Kramer
Chief Sub-Editor: Ilse Gray

Chief of Editorial Production: Jane Hawker
Production Assistants: Alan Godwin, Maureen Kelly
Editorial Department: Theresa John, Debra Lelliott,
Sylvia Osborne

Series Editor: Tony Allan

Editorial Staff for *Italy*
Editor: Gillian Moore
Researcher: Lesley Coleman
Designer: Lynne Brown
Sub-Editor: Sally Rowland
Picture Department: Christine Hinze, Peggy Tout
Editorial Assistant: Molly Oates

Contributors: The chapter texts were written by: Iain
Carson, Frederic V. Grunfeld, Robert Harvey and Alan
Lothian.

Correspondents: Elisabeth Kraemer-Singh (Bonn);
Dorothy Bacon (London); Maria Vincenza Aloisi,
Josephine du Brusle (Paris); Ann Natanson (Rome).
Valuable assistance was also provided by: Bona Schmid,
Anna Polo (Milan).

CONSULTANTS

Dr. Denis Mack Smith is Senior Research Fellow
of All Souls College, Oxford. He has written
many books on modern Italian history. John
Haycraft, Director-General of International
House, a worldwide group of English-language
schools, has recently completed a book on modern Italy entitled *Italian Labyrinth*.

PHOTOGRAPHER

Romano Cagnoni was born in Tuscany but since
1958 he has lived in London. Journalistic assign-
ments have taken him to most of the world's
troublespots, including Biafra, Vietnam, Af-
ghanistan and the Middle East. He has also pho-
tographed many aspects of his native Italy.
He travelled in Italy for three months to shoot
the photographs for this volume in the Library
of Nations series.

ISBN 0-8094-5311-8 (lib. bdg.)

Library of Congress Catalogue Card Number: 86-60310

Edime Org. Gráfica, S. A.
Móstoles (Madrid)

Depósito Legal: M. 15.643-1986
I.S.B.N.: 84-599-1419-4

IMPRESO EN ESPAÑA
PRINTED IN SPAIN

COVER: Arcaded palaces flank Venice's main
thoroughfare, the Grand Canal, where gondolas
lie moored between their posts.

PAGES 1 AND 2: The emblem on page 1 includes a star, representing the Italian nation, su-
perimposed on a cogwheel, standing for labour,
and framed by branches of oak and olive,
which indicate strength and peace respectively.
Italy's national flag, a tricolour in green, white
and red, is shown on the following page.

FRONT AND BACK ENDPAPERS: A topo-
graphic map showing the major rivers, mountain ranges and other natural features of
Italy appears on the front endpaper; the back
endpaper shows the country's 20 regions and
principal towns.

This volume is one in a series of books describing countries of the world — their natural
resources, peoples, histories, economies and governments.

CONTENTS

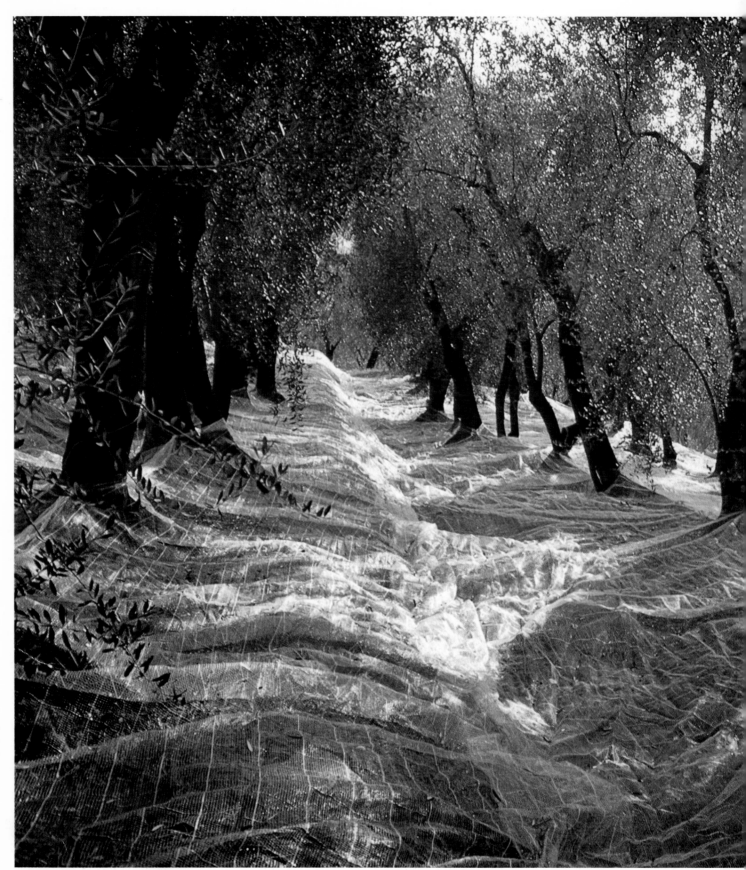

Pale November sunlight filters through a grove of Tuscan olive trees on to nets spread out to catch the ripe fruit when the branches are shaken. The olive

6

has for centuries been an agricultural staple in Italy, which vies with Spain to produce the world's largest annual olive-oil yield.

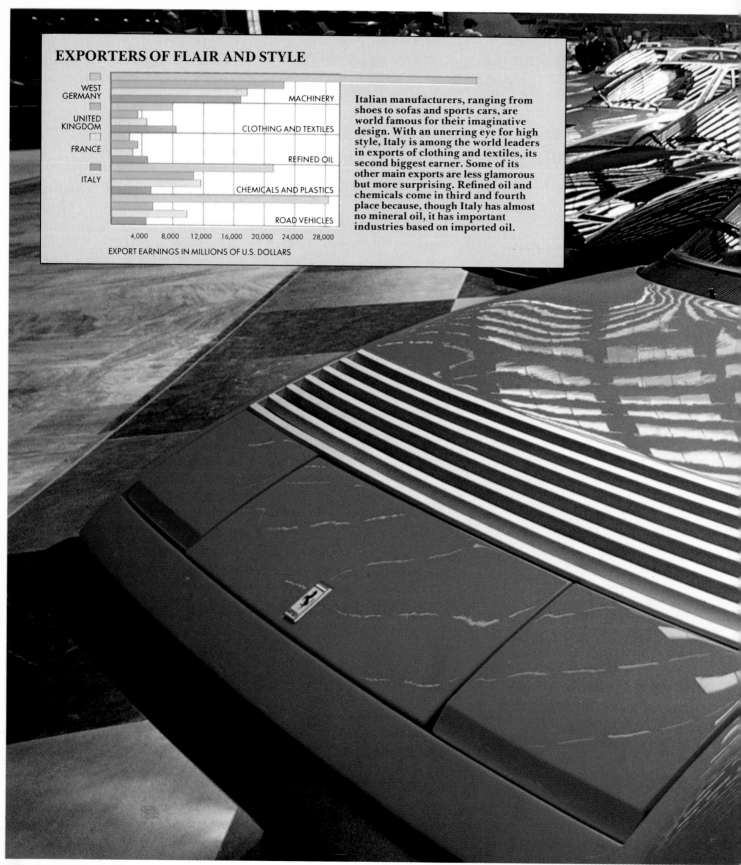

EXPORTERS OF FLAIR AND STYLE

	MACHINERY
WEST GERMANY	
UNITED KINGDOM	CLOTHING AND TEXTILES
FRANCE	REFINED OIL
ITALY	CHEMICALS AND PLASTICS
	ROAD VEHICLES

4,000 8,000 12,000 16,000 20,000 24,000 28,000

EXPORT EARNINGS IN MILLIONS OF U.S. DOLLARS

Italian manufacturers, ranging from shoes to sofas and sports cars, are world famous for their imaginative design. With an unerring eye for high style, Italy is among the world leaders in exports of clothing and textiles, its second biggest earner. Some of its other main exports are less glamorous but more surprising. Refined oil and chemicals come in third and fourth place because, though Italy has almost no mineral oil, it has important industries based on imported oil.

A Ferrari painted gleaming scarlet—the traditional Italian colour at international motor races—reflects the overhead lights at the biennial Turin car show.

8

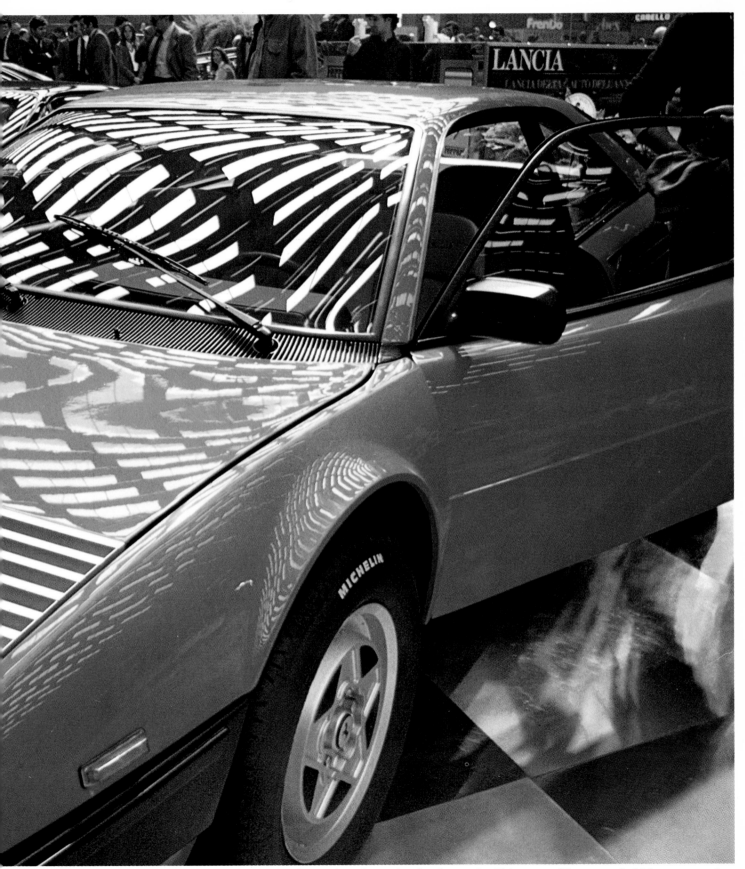

Sports-car manufacturers such as Maserati, Lamborghini and Ferrari produce only a few thousand vehicles a year, 80 per cent of which are exported.

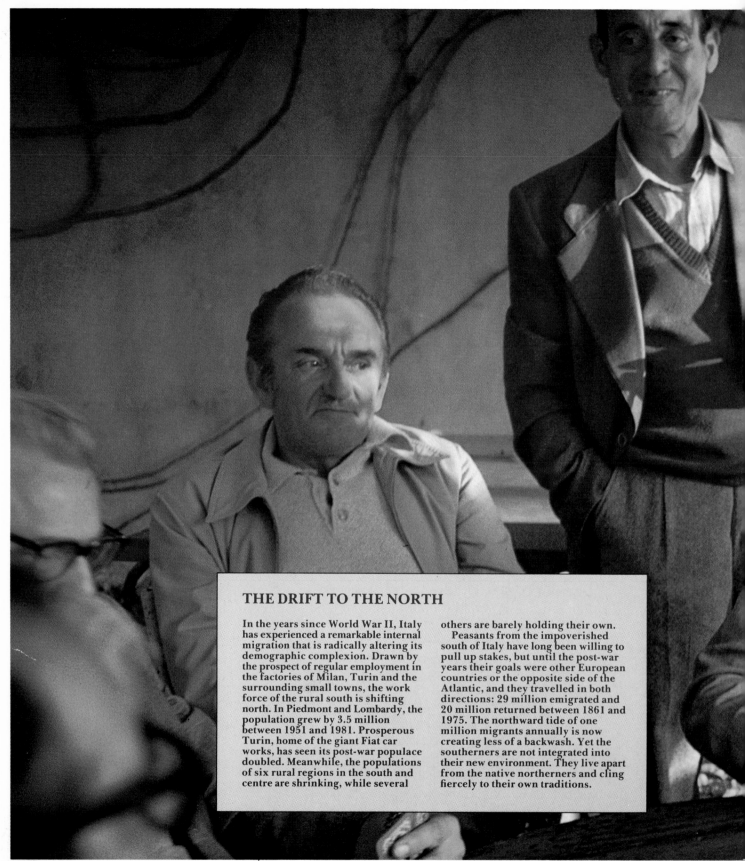

THE DRIFT TO THE NORTH

In the years since World War II, Italy has experienced a remarkable internal migration that is radically altering its demographic complexion. Drawn by the prospect of regular employment in the factories of Milan, Turin and the surrounding small towns, the work force of the rural south is shifting north. In Piedmont and Lombardy, the population grew by 3.5 million between 1951 and 1981. Prosperous Turin, home of the giant Fiat car works, has seen its post-war populace doubled. Meanwhile, the populations of six rural regions in the south and centre are shrinking, while several others are barely holding their own.

Peasants from the impoverished south of Italy have long been willing to pull up stakes, but until the post-war years their goals were other European countries or the opposite side of the Atlantic, and they travelled in both directions: 29 million emigrated and 20 million returned between 1861 and 1975. The northward tide of one million migrants annually is now creating less of a backwash. Yet the southerners are not integrated into their new environment. They live apart from the native northerners and cling fiercely to their own traditions.

Scrutinized by a cluster of companions, southern-bred workers play cards in a garden in Valletta, a migrants' suburb outside Turin. Short-sighted urban planning has left immigrants to the industrial north crowded into shanty towns—enclaves of clannish Mediterranean life in the heart of modern Italy.

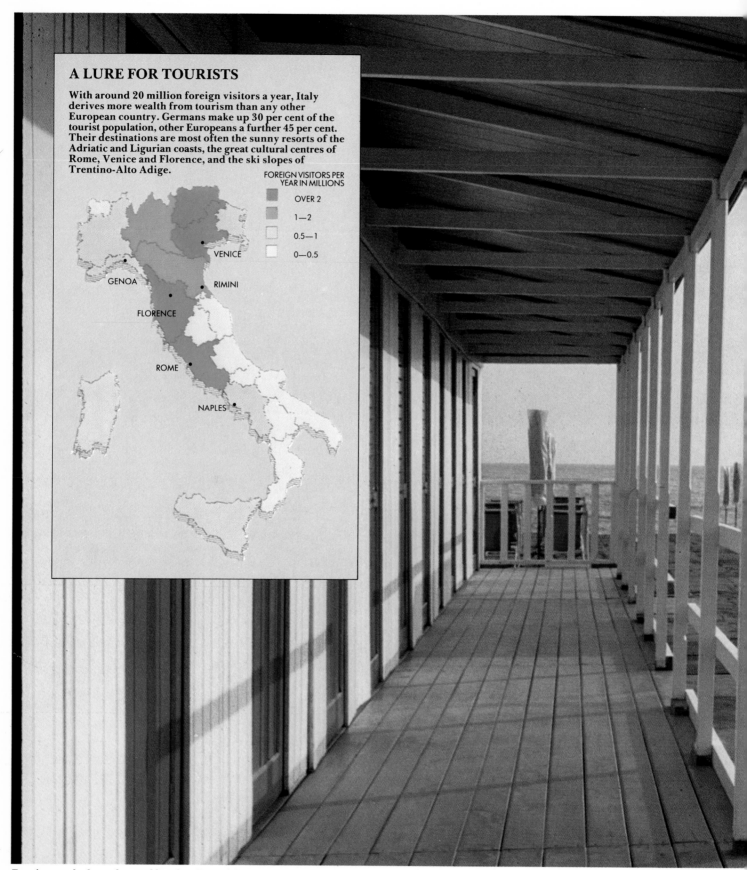

A LURE FOR TOURISTS

With around 20 million foreign visitors a year, Italy derives more wealth from tourism than any other European country. Germans make up 30 per cent of the tourist population, other Europeans a further 45 per cent. Their destinations are most often the sunny resorts of the Adriatic and Ligurian coasts, the great cultural centres of Rome, Venice and Florence, and the ski slopes of Trentino-Alto Adige.

FOREIGN VISITORS PER YEAR IN MILLIONS

- OVER 2
- 1—2
- 0.5—1
- 0—0.5

VENICE

GENOA

RIMINI

FLORENCE

ROME

NAPLES

Evening sun bathes a deserted beach at Forte dei Marmi on the Tuscan coast. At the end of the afternoon when the holidaymakers decamp, beach attendants

clear the litter, rake the sand and straighten the deckchairs in readiness for the next day's onslaught.

A SPORTING MANIA

The Italians adore football with a passion that is matched in few other countries. More than a quarter of a million spectators watch first division matches live, and many thousands more devotedly attend the games of the other three divisions and the countless clashes between amateur teams. No fewer than three national daily papers are dedicated exclusively to sport—chiefly football—and on Mondays, after the big matches, serious newspapers devote half their pages to the game. Footballers are among the highest-paid employees in the country, and Italian clubs have attracted a high proportion of the world's best players.

One reason for the excitement generated by the game is the strength of regional loyalties. Italy only became a unified state in 1861, and ancient rivalries between the city-states that made up the peninsula have never been forgotten. They are revived by every confrontation in the stadiums—whether between neighbouring towns' teams or giants such as Roma and Turin's Juventus.

Lines of red shirts belonging to members of a local football club hang out to dry in a garden in Cortona, Tuscany. Because of a shortage of grassy pitches

Italian amateur players often practise on asphalt, and thereby learn the fast ball control and tricky manoeuvres that are a hallmark of the national style.

1

Before sitting down to a festive lunch, a proud Sicilian family smiles for the photograph that will commemorate a daughter's first communion. About 60 per cent of Italian children still take this step—usually at eight—though nowadays less than a third of the population attend church regularly.

THE STRENGTH OF THE FAMILY

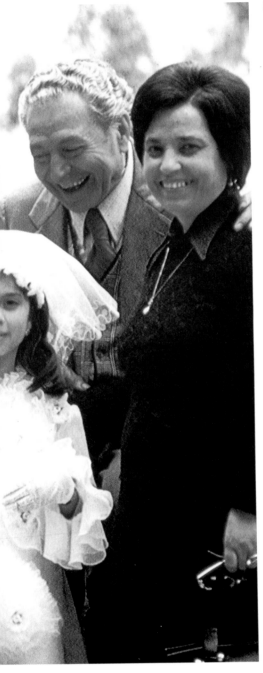

"*Povera Italia*," the Italians like to say, especially after a good meal with good friends. The food has been, as always, excellent, the wine clean and delicious. So it ought to be, the guests are assured: it was made in the cellar of the host's brother-in-law's uncle. A little *grappa* —a spirit distilled from grape stalks and skins—may be offered round with the coffee. It too is wholesome and genuine, as indeed it was bound to be, since the man who distilled it is the host's wife's second cousin.

"Poor Italy," the guests agree, and settle down to an enthusiastic conversation on the trials and tribulations of Italian daily life. The current scandal afflicting the government is a certain topic; the near-impossibility of a speedy or intelligent service from the state-owned power or telephone company; the flagrant way a local politician is handing out contracts to relatives and supporters; the fantastic delays in postal services. Perhaps another *grappa*? The guests decline. They have a long way to drive home along the auto-strada; and conversation turns for a moment to a comparison between the latest Alfa-Romeo and the newest Lancia. To some of the guests, neither car is out of reach.

Not so long ago, Italy—or large portions of it anyway—was genuinely poor. As late as 1951 it was predominantly an agricultural country, with more than 40 per cent of the labour force working on the land. It was pros-

perous, for the most part, in the north; almost wealthy, even, around the few industrial cities. But the south was trapped in deep poverty and nowhere, north or south, did Italy's standard of living seriously compare with its Western European neighbours. In 1953, a Parliamentary Commission on poverty reported that 24 per cent of Italian households were either "destitute" or "in hardship"; that there was overcrowding in 21 per cent of dwellings; that 52 per cent of homes in the south were without running drinking water and only 57 per cent had a lavatory. Rocketing growth rates in the 1950s and 1960s (exceeded only by Japan's) changed all that, and Italy is now a thriving industrial state.

Measured by almost every index of well-being, the Italians are better off than most of them imagined possible. They eat better; they have better education; fewer of their babies die and most adults live longer. In the crasser terms of consumer goods—telephones, cars, washing machines and television sets—Italian ownership approaches, matches and sometimes even exceeds the Western European average. True, the well-being is not evenly spread: discrepancies between rich and poor are high by European standards and the south still lags well behind the north, but even there things have improved out of all recognition.

The Italians have not only achieved the most astounding economic trans-

1

formation in Western Europe: they have managed something perhaps more difficult. They have retained a great many of the civilized habits of everyday life that have long attracted outsiders to their land. They care about good food and good wine not only for their own sakes, but on account of the fellowship and conversation that go with them. They like to talk: Italian bars, for instance, are noted more for animated discussion than serious drinking; and on market day in a small community the cumulative murmur of townsfolk simply chattering—rarely shouting—can be deafening.

Every day the social network is reinforced by the great Italian institution of the *passeggiata*, a kind of mass stroll that takes place in most small towns and many large ones in the early evening. It is at once a fashion parade for the young and a little light exercise for the elderly, a chance for town-wide gossip, an unstructured appointment system and an opportunity to renew acquaintanceship. With a wave, a handshake, a friendly clasp on the shoulder, neighbours can be seen dispensing affection and goodwill. An outsider in an Italian community almost inevitably comes away with an impression of a stable, vigorous and well-knit society.

Yet with so much to be glad about, Italians persist in lamenting their country's failings. An opinion survey carried out in the mid-1980s throughout the European Community revealed that only 6 per cent of Italians counted themselves "very happy": no other country except Greece scored so low. Most Italians would describe themselves as fatalists rather than pessimists; they may, indeed, be the most contented people in the world, though superstitiously convinced that to admit it would bring bad luck. But their woes are real enough; life can be difficult indeed in one of the richest industrial countries in the world.

To begin with, there is the chronic weakness of Italian governments, which makes the economic miracle of the post-war decades seem more than usually miraculous. An achievement of such magnitude is more easily understood where there is a stable and efficient, even authoritarian state working in harmonious consensus with an energetic, disciplined people; Germany is an obvious example. Yet the Italian economic feat is even more remarkable than Germany's post-war recovery. The two countries' economies grew at about the same rate in the 1950s, but in the 1960s, when Germany's growth slowed down a little, Italy's accelerated, reaching an annual average of over 6 per cent during the whole second half of the decade. In order to achieve this remarkable result, the Italians have had to make do with little more than their own astonishing dynamism.

Since its foundation in 1946, the Italian Republic has had over 40 governments, some lasting less than a month. Such transience in the corridors of power is by no means the symptom of instability that it at first appears, since every government has been a coalition dominated by the Christian Democrat Party, and each government has contained most of the same ministers—perhaps in different ministries -as its predecessor; but most coalitions have spent more time locked in internal wrangling than they have governing the country. Laws minor or major have inevitably been compromises, and sometimes so badly drafted that they are almost impossible to implement—if, that is, a reliable way of implementing them even existed.

For the administration of the Italian state is a byword for delay, complexity and sheer incompetence. A country can easily live with rapidly changing governments if it is equipped with a good civil service: France in the 1950s, for example, was characterized by a worse-than-Italian chaos in government while an icily efficient and superbly

Seen through mist, the hilltop town of San Gimignano bristles with towers. Family pride was measured there in the Middle Ages by the height of rival households' dwellings. The town was top-heavy with some 76 turrets when, in the 14th century, city fathers put a ceiling on the height limit.

trained administrative system saw to it that the nation carried on regardless with its post-war reconstruction. But in Italy the administration is out of control. Government spends more than 50 per cent of the gross national product, and misuses a large proportion of that colossal sum.

A 1984 report on the near-paralysis of the Italian civil service by the Formez Research Institute needed 14,000 pages to do justice to its subject. Its painstaking authors found terrifying examples of waste and delay. Take the small farmer whose crops had been ruined by hail. He sought one of the emergency loans offered by a benevolent government, and he got it—almost three years later, after his application had been processed by no fewer than 10 different offices. Or consider the war widow who had to spend decades queuing and enduring bureaucratic rebuffs before she obtained her

meagre pension. Most Italians, who have to deal with the system with distressing frequency in the course of their lives, could recount similar stories.

The investigators discovered a backlog of 450,000 outstanding files in Rome's Treasury Ministry alone, and everywhere a bloated work force who arrived late and left early—usually to go on to a second job. There is no sign that things are likely to get much better; indeed, since Italy's bureaucrats have been buying job-lots of computers with scarcely an attempt to fit them into a logical work-system, there is every likelihood that things will get much worse.

The judicial system is in even more grave condition. Occasionally outright chicanery weakens faith in its integrity; more damagingly still, its desperate slowness destroys faith in its utility. Prisoners without the means or friends and relatives to make a public nuisance of themselves sometimes spend many years in jail awaiting trial; civil suits in the 1970s could expect a waiting time of 10 years or so and, despite attempts to streamline procedures, delays of three or four years were commonplace a decade later.

The educational system also has major defects. Compulsory schooling runs only from age six to 14, but most children stay on longer in the often-disappointed hope of a better job—or any job at all. And while expenditure on education has risen steadily over the years, almost all the money has been spent on staff, so that, although Italy can claim the most favourable teacher-pupil ratio in the European Community, schools are often overcrowded and woefully underequipped.

In the south, where the problem is most acute, many schools operate a two-shift system with quite distinct sets of pupils and teachers in the mornings and afternoons. Almost everywhere, instruction is uninspired and routine. Science teaching is often rudimentary, and children are ill-prepared to enter a rapidly changing industrial society. "The curriculum goes back at least 40 years," said one disillusioned teacher in Naples. "Old-fashioned rote learn-ing: it's completely out of touch with what the kids need, and what's more the kids know it." She added, bitterly, "For them, school has become no more than a parking place between childhood and unemployment."

Universities are grossly over-crowded as well, because there is no ceiling imposed on student numbers. They produce hordes of arts graduates at the expense of much-needed scien-tists and engineers. Such an ill-balanced output is one of the reasons for Italy's high teacher–pupil ratio, but even an overstaffed education system

In towns the length of Italy, balconies serve as forums for gossip and observation posts from which to scan the bustle of neighbourhood life. They also provide cramped apartment dwellers with a welcome modicum of extra space for plants and laundry.

and a swollen public service between them are unable to absorb the flood of degree-waving hopefuls. Italy suffers from a steadily worsening problem of graduate unemployment. The authorities worry about the political discontent that it generates, but they do not take any action.

The universities also produce more medical practitioners than most other countries. Italy's health service is not short-staffed, but the salaries of medical personnel and administrators swallow up far too large a proportion of the funds available. In parts of the south, hospital patients often have to rely on relatives for food and clean linen. In Milan, at the hub of Italian prosperity, it is not unheard of for major hospitals to close their doors to emergency admissions while the staff struggle with a backlog of patients crammed into dirty corridors in camp-beds.

Other welfare services are no more enviable. Until the mid-1970s, social security was practically non-existent. Unemployment pay is still derisory and, although old-age pensions have vastly increased, actually obtaining one can involve a citizen in a prolonged and exhausting struggle with a notoriously unhelpful officialdom.

And over the whole massive shambles of the Italian state hangs the unedifying aroma of corruption. A selection of newspaper stories that were published over one summer month in the mid-1980s is representative of what goes on all the time. One sequence of articles concerned a crisis in the government: a minister had been accused of belonging to a secret Masonic society whose least sinister purpose appeared to be the enrichment of its members. Then there was a report from Spain: Italian magistrates were strug-

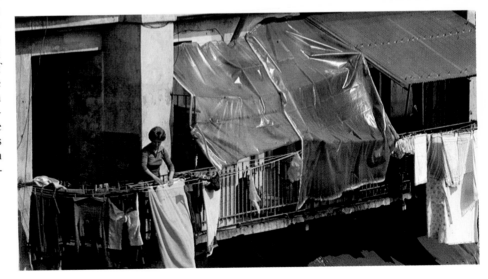

1

gling to extradite an ex-General of Italy's Financial Police, who was wanted for his part in a multibillion lira revenue fraud. Simultaneously, correspondents on the island of Sicily sent news of a government inspector whose duty was to ensure that wine and food-stuffs were not adulterated by sharp operators—who had himself been arrested for adulteration.

These were only the few who had been caught out. The newspapers also presented a sober report on outrageous under-declarations of income to the tax authorities by small businesses and members of the professions: the fashionable Roman bars whose official turnover amounted to no more than 40 ice-creams a day; the successful lawyers who mysteriously earned less than a third of their office rentals. The government of the day was engaged in trying to stamp out tax fraud, but such stories show how colossal a task it had set itself. And as a crowning irony, the newspapers announced that the Pope had just awarded a prize to a theologian who declared that hell indeed existed, but might well be empty. It came as no surprise to cynical Italians: even in the next world, they knew the rascals would get away with it.

Anywhere else, such a background of institutional chaos and corruption would signify not the brink of disaster but disaster itself, a country plunging into ruin and misery. Yet Italians are not merely surviving but flourishing. The observer finds himself asking two questions. The first is obvious: how do they manage so well? The second follows when the stranger has realized that Italians are not the crazy, easygoing romantics of legend, but a tough, shrewd and hard-headed people. At

that point he wants to know: why on earth do they choose to put up with such a situation?

Both questions share a single answer and it lies in one institution in which Italians do place their faith. It is an institution with no headquarters building and no supporting bureaucracy. It protects Italians from misgovernment even as it ensures that misgovernment is inevitable. That institution is the family. Its members not only sustain one another with supplies of home-made wine and *grappa*, but with assiduous manoeuvring to protect one another's interests in the outside world.

The key position of the family in Italian life is largely the result of the nation's turbulent history. Nominally united under the Romans, the Italian peninsula was fragmented by the fourth century A.D., and for the next 13 centuries large parts of it fell under foreign rule. Arbitrary and corrupt government by unsympathetic strangers was the lot of most Italians; and wars were all too frequent. The unification of Italy in 1861 did very little to increase ordinary Italians' involvement with their state. The vote was denied to illiterates—who made up two-thirds of the population.

To the poverty-stricken southerners, especially, parliament seemed remote and irrelevant, and in the course of the 1860s the south was torn by guerrilla warfare and bloody uprisings. In the 20th century, under Mussolini, Italy experienced strong centralized government for the first time since the Roman Empire—but the excesses of fascism traumatized the nation even more than centuries of misrule by foreigners.

With so little experience of wise and just government, Italians have naturally turned to smaller, domestic units

for their everyday succour and support. To an Italian, the family is a fortress, a defended position within which the virtues of loyalty, probity, discipline, foresight and self-sacrifice—all of them sadly lacking in Italy's public life—are exercised almost automatically. The family is also a vehicle for progress—its own progress.

And there lies the rub. What benefits one family does not necessarily benefit all the others: the idea of the general good has never taken deep root in Italy. Authority is rarely respected in its own, abstract right. The agencies of the state, far from representing impersonal pillars of national administration, are merely examples of someone else's family getting ahead. Those in positions of power, the winning players in the great game, have to be treated with respect, placated if necessary and deceived if possible by other, lesser players who are seeking advantage for their own families.

Hence the apparent shamelessness of much of Italian public life, and the relative tolerance extended to corrupt officials. In many Italians, outrage is blended with a sneaking admiration. On a much smaller scale, indeed, most of them play the same game. Any self-respecting family can lay claim to some sort of network of contacts, without which the simplest transactions—especially those involving the state bureaucracy—can be both exhausting and time-consuming. One southerner, busily engaged in favour-trading to acquire the recommendation from a local politician that would ensure his son a job, explained the Catch-22 reasoning that has kept the system alive so long. "Of course it would be better for everybody if nobody did this sort of thing," he said. "But everybody who can,

Completely absorbed in each other's company, mothers and sons of two generations stroll beside the Grand Canal in Venice. The powerful bond forged between a young boy and his mother does not diminish even when the son stands a head taller than his elderly *mamma*.

1

does—so what do you expect from me? Listen, my boy needs that job."

But if the system generates public anarchy, it also creates a good deal of private stability. Family life, after all, is the bedrock of all human societies; and habits of decency at home provide at least some moderating influence on public excesses. Take, for example, the hosts we encountered earlier enjoying a *grappa* with their guests. The older members of that household will remember the extended family life that prevailed in Italy until a generation ago. They may romanticize the past a little, recalling how children, parents and grandparents all lived together, sharing a joint livelihood, meeting two or three times a day for meals that were really social sacraments presided over by a twinkling-eyed patriarch with a notoriously soft spot for the young. They will not, however, forget the squalor of overcrowding and the sheer brutal labour that was the lot of the great majority.

In today's easier circumstances, Italy is becoming a nation of nuclear families: fewer than 10 per cent of households have over five members. But our hosts most probably still live near their parents and visit them regularly. Their sense of family solidarity, of shared goals, of respect for elders and love for children will be as strong as anything their parents felt.

Italians take children seriously, and they take boy-children especially seriously, because the family is male-orientated—though not, perhaps, as male-dominated as most outsiders and many Italian men imagine it to be. Certainly, the boy-child is treated as a little king—spoiled, flattered, encouraged to be articulate, and continually assured of his own charm. He will grow up,

with any luck, into a self-confident, sensitive young man; his sensitivity, though likely to include an excessive fear of ridicule, of making a fool of himself, will allow him a closer and easier relationship with women than men of northern nations can usually manage. This is one of his mother's gifts to him—one of many, for in Italy a son is his mother's masterpiece.

The bond between Italian men and their mothers is probably, for good or ill, the most powerful social tie in the country, and it has led to the somewhat startling phenomenon of *mammismo*. The word is impossible to translate and the concept behind it difficult to elucidate. It describes both the lifelong need of a man for the kind of maternal attention he was given in childhood, as well as the even greater need felt by many mothers to continue to provide it. It accounts for the immense influence Italian women have usually been able to wield in an ostensibly patriarchal society where their legal rights until recently were very much less extensive than those of their men.

Indeed, if an Italian boy is raised as a king, a little girl is trained from birth to be the quiet power behind the throne. She is taught to be self-effacing, less extrovert than her brother, even secretive. Her role is to be that of wife and eventually mother, bringing up her own sons in turn as the family's greatest glory while she passes on to her daughters the legacy of quiet cunning and moral toughness that actually holds the family together.

The harder the family situation, the tougher the Italian women become; and the more obvious the apparent patriarchy, the more developed the matriarchal sinews underneath. In rural southern Italy, for example, women

are ostensibly little more than appendages of their husbands and fathers, and often they are beasts of burden to boot. Yet acute observers have noted that it is the women who take the real decisions in most communities, who keep them functioning in conditions of grinding poverty that send their men helplessly to the wineshops, there to grumble in despair.

In gentler circumstances, when they can afford to look beyond mere survival, Italian women set much store by family meals. Italians spend a higher proportion of their incomes on food than do other industrialized nations. Every housewife who can will shop frequently, putting a premium on freshness; the food she prepares will be simple, plentiful and excellent. Respect for meals is reflected in working hours throughout most of Italy, especially in the hotter climate of the south: shops and offices close for anything up to four hours in the middle of the day, allowing everybody time for a long nap after a substantial lunch.

Sons and daughters who have left home come back for regular family gatherings and, since most dwellings are too small for entertaining on a large scale, restaurants do good business. Nephews, nieces, uncles, aunts and cousins and various generations may well appear round the table: a good family party is a big family party.

Through institutions such as the extended family gathering and the evening stroll, Italy's millions of family "nation-states" ensure that they do not exist in isolation. Like real "nation-states", each family binds itself to others by webs of alliance spun from mutual interest. Although each is willing to stretch and twist the fabric of Italian society to achieve its own ends, it is in the interests of none to destroy the fabric altogether.

Had any wished to do so, it would have found a formidable opponent in the self-proclaimed defender of the family, the Roman Catholic Church. The role of the Church in Italian political and social history has been profound. To Italians, the papacy is almost a national institution. Apart from seven turbulent decades in the 14th century, when the popes resided in Avignon, the head of the Catholic Church has always been based in Rome. Moreover, until 1870 part of the country was under direct papal rule. Throughout the peninsula, the Church provided the only social services Italians of past generations knew; it still supplements the state-provided health and welfare services. Religious orders run some of the best schools in the country, which are patronized by the affluent élite. In the rural communities of the past, the parish priest was the natural leader, the man to whom families turned with problems and questions of all kinds. Even today, the Church's moral authority remains tremendous.

Italian society has needed all the strength at its disposal to withstand the buffetings of the last few decades. The transformation of a deeply traditional, agrarian people into a thriving, dynamic industrial state compressed into three short decades a social evolution that elsewhere in Europe took at least a century. The Big Bang, one writer called it, with pardonable hyperbole, and Italians still hear the ringing in their ears.

For millions of families, economic growth has meant a traumatic move from the countryside to the cities—above all from the countryside of the south to the cities of the north. Since 1951, about 10 million people (six million according to notoriously unreliable government statistics and at least double that figure according to some informed observers) have uprooted themselves from the land and settled in Turin, Milan and the other industrial centres. The traditions of family life were a product of the old, agricultural Italy, an Italy of poverty and hardship,

EATING WELL ALLA ITALIANA

A market stall is piled high with dried beans.

Salami in all shapes and sizes hang in a Tuscan food shop.

A modern ice-cream parlour displays its range of flavours.

Chili peppers glow beside olives picked at every stage of ripeness.

Shoppers contemplate festooned ranks of Italian cheeses.

A *pasticceria* offers a selection of cakes, pastries and sweetmeats.

Good food is one of life's great pleasures for the Italians, who show their appreciation in the clearest way. Proportionately, they spend more of their income on food than any Western European country.

It is not that they have lavish tastes; pasta, the closest thing to a national dish, is one of the most economical of foods. Pasta or a rice dish rarely fails to appear in one form or another in a typical family meal. Usually it will be followed by meat or fish, vegetables—which the Italians eat in greater quantities than any other people in Europe—a salad, and fruit or cheese. Elaborate desserts seldom appear on the family table, although it is customary for guests to bring a cake bought from one of the excellent pastry shops to be found throughout the country.

What distinguishes such a meal is the quality and freshness of its ingredients. Good cooking starts in the marketplace, which most Italian cooks visit daily. Frozen and canned foods have little place in the kitchen, and the supermarket has yet to replace the family stall or small shop offering farm fruit and vegetables. As a result, Italy has Europe's highest number of food retail outlets—more than four times as many as West Germany, for example.

The markets also display in profusion the preserved foods—hams, sausages, cheeses and dried pulses—which even in the recent past were an essential means of storing summer's plenty against winter's dearth. Many of them are prepared by time-consuming methods and are priced accordingly; Parmesan cheese, for example, is aged for two to four years, and the most mature is considered the choicest. For foodwise Italians, using cheaper substitutes would be an affront to tradition and their own discriminating tastes.

small towns and stubborn peasant farmers. The migrants to the cities have been hard-put to retain them.

In the early days of the great industrialization, rural menfolk often set off alone to seek factory jobs. They lived in barrack-like conditions in northern cities, sending most of their new wages to their women and children in the home villages. Normal family living was impossible but men and women alike had the consolation that the sacrifices were for the good of the family, that, however agonizing the experience, they were making progress.

By the late 1960s, however, with waves of immigrants still flooding into the jerry-built slums that had been erected around the periphery of the northern cities, the novelty of regular earnings had worn off, and with it a good deal of the initial optimism. Wages were not high, job security was minimal and state welfare benefits practically non-existent. The old supportive networks of extended family relationships had been shrivelled by their translation to ill-planned overcrowded cities. The sharply differentiated roles of men and women, which had seemed inevitable in a rural community, made much less sense in industrial cities. The younger generation had neither memories of the old ways to sustain it nor a secure place in the new industrial society to compensate. Strains within families multiplied, and losses began to outweigh gains.

There arose a two-fold dissatisfaction with the brash consumer society that had come into being in little more than a decade. On the one hand, a great many ordinary people saw themselves excluded from a fair share in the well-being they were creating. On the other, a new generation of the educated young

rejected the consumer society entirely and demanded nothing less than a revolution.

The spectacle of student revolt was by no means confined to Italy, of course. In most Western countries, 1968 was a heady year for privileged youth. But in Italy, the *sessantottini*—the "sixty-eighters", as a whole generation of more-or-less radicalized young intellectuals would be called—came of age in a society already in turmoil as a result of the rapid social changes it was living through. Some of the sixty-eighters were prepared to go a good deal further than their fellow radicals in other countries.

The means by which the extremists sought to topple what they regarded as a hopelessly corrupt state were assassinations, bombings and kidnappings. They began in 1968 and reached a peak 10 years later, in 1978, with the kidnapping and murder of former prime minister Aldo Moro by terrorists belonging to the Marxist Red Brigades. The Italian police at first seemed powerless to deal with the menace.

But the murder of Aldo Moro—not to mention close to 2,500 other terrorist attacks that year—galvanized the Italian authorities into effective action. Just as importantly, it sickened the Italian public. Efficient policework and a new public commitment to co-operation with the authorities crippled the terrorists. The fabric of society turned out to be stronger than the terrorists had imagined.

One of the reasons for its strength was that other campaigns succeeded in transforming society by peaceful means. The 1970s saw a vast rise in the real incomes of most ordinary Italians as well as the enactment of secure-employment legislation and at last the creation of a welfare state of sorts. It was a stormy decade, by any standards, and it inspired plenty of gloom-laden writing from commentators both inside and outside the country. Yet Italy was clearly in better shape at the end of it than at its beginning.

Women, for example, were no longer obviously second-class citizens. More of them were now going out to work. Peasant women always had, of course; but, in the north especially, women were taking jobs at all levels in the Italian economy, in a pattern that quite closely reflected the other Western European countries. Around a quarter of Italian doctors are now women, for example—a figure that would have been unthinkable in the immediate

post-war years.

Legislation passed in the late 1960s and the 1970s was at last giving them rights that at least partly matched their husbands'. A law allowing an adulterous wife to be imprisoned was repealed, for instance; married women were given control over their own property; and working women were granted five months of maternity leave on full pay. It will take time for these changes in the law to gradually work their way through to everyday family life. But even in the south, where traditions die hardest, the old male-dominated ways cannot last forever.

Perhaps the most startling developments of all, in a country where 97 per cent of the population are baptized

Catholics, were the legalization of divorce in 1970 and abortion in 1978 despite the implacable opposition of the Church. Such reforms were partly the result of declining ecclesiastical influence: only around 30 per cent of the population attend church regularly, compared with nearly 60 per cent in the 1950s. Perhaps, too, they were possible because Italians have long learnt not to take tirades from the pulpit too seriously: they have lived with the Church for centuries, after all, and although they will listen respectfully to what their parish priest has to say to them, they are prepared on occasion to choose their own way afterwards.

The delay in legalizing divorce stemmed from the fact that the interests of the Church and those of Italian families coincided: Italian women, especially, were suspicious that divorce would simply allow their husbands to throw them out with no financial support. Yet the dire predictions made by the Church, that divorce would be the death of the Italian family, have not been borne out by experience. After an initial surge, the Italian divorce rate had settled down by the early 1980s to 13,000 a year—0.2 per thousand inhabitants, compared with 2.8 per thousand in Britain and 1.7 per thousand in Catholic France.

In the case of abortion, the law merely recognized an existing state of affairs. Contrary to the Church's teaching, Italians have always practised it, along with whatever other methods of birth control were available. The rate of abortion is now the highest in Europe after Denmark. But Italians have never seen abortion or contraception as threats to family life. Instead, they are thought to strengthen it, by reducing illegitimate births and encouraging small families in which each child can be sure of the cosseting that Italians like to give their offspring.

Although the new laws may not be responsible for undermining the social order, there is evidence of something seriously amiss in the Italian family, and it comes in the form of drug-taking. Since the mid-1970s, the strains of rapid social change have been augmented by the same alarming youth unemployment that afflicts most of the world's developed nations. When even the most assiduously cultivated family connections are insufficient to find a job, many youngsters seek escape through drugs.

Though the problem may be understandable, its extent is extremely worrying. In the early 1980s, there were 20,000 heroin addicts registered with the authorities in Italy, compared with 30,000 in West Germany and 10,000 in Britain. But the registered addicts are only a fraction of the total, and in Italy they seem to be a smaller fraction than elsewhere. Surveys and hearsay, admittedly unreliable, suggest that the situation in Italy is actually more serious than elsewhere in Europe—and deteriorating sharply following the fall in heroin prices of the mid-1980s.

Drug addiction is not restricted to any one region or social class. It is as much a menace in southern cities, where traditional attitudes supposedly still prevail, as it is in the big northern metropolises with their uprooted, immigrant populations. University students and the unemployed in the slums are almost equally at risk: the only common factor seems to be the youth of the victims, for practically all are under 30. And drug-taking on this scale is not only a symptom of social stress: it is also a prime cause of it. At the very least it breeds lawlessness, as addicts turn to crime in order to feed their expensive habit. By the early 1980s, 30 per cent of Italy's prison population—itself high by European standards, at 43,000—were addicts.

One of the most alarming aspects of the problem is the speed with which it has developed in Italy. Explains Nicola Dellisanti, one of the organizers of a nationwide drug rehabilitation scheme, "Up until 1972 or 1973, drug-taking here was insignificant. We were a conduit in the international drug trade, perhaps. But never a market." So why the explosion? "I'd say 50 per cent because of the crisis young Italians are going through: a crisis of traditional values, a crisis in the family generally, little crises in lots of families. Despair." And the other 50 per cent? "Because suddenly the drugs were there." And so, he might have added, was the money to buy them.

It is a bitter irony that the source of all these family-wrecking narcotics is itself a family business—the world's most sinister. The Mafia, in fact, represents the idea of family loyalty taken to a murderous extreme. It is in many ways a dark mirror in which the image of Italian society at large is reflected, horribly distorted but not unrecognizable; and since society has been busily transforming itself, so has the Mafia.

Like the rest of Italian society, the Mafia has deep, traditional roots. It began in western Sicily, which is still its heartland, and at first it was more a manner of behaviour than anything as structured as a secret criminal organization. Law and order in that turbulent and roadless province were almost non-existent: in order to avoid being swallowed up in the general turmoil, a man had to be ready to avenge any slight, real or imagined, to his own honour or that of his family.

To make oneself respected in the community—that was what counted.

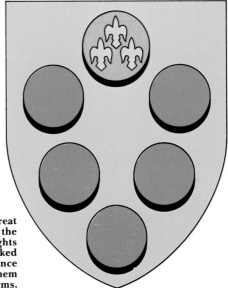

The six orbs on the arms of the great Renaissance banking family, the Medici, are said to represent weights with which moneychangers checked coins. A 16th-century king of France honoured the Medici by letting them use three lilies from his own arms.

1

The more violence a man was prepared to use, the more respect he enjoyed, and murder became a high road to social advancement. In the continued absence of effective government, ordinary people began to turn to the local "man of respect" with their questions and problems, thus increasing his power. Conflicts between men of respect themselves required the emergence of men of even greater respect to resolve them, and a loose, shifting hierarchy gradually evolved.

The unification of Italy enhanced rather than weakened the position of the Sicilian *mafiosi*. For the most part, the state virtually delegated its powers to them; the Mafia, after all, could be relied upon to deliver votes, and the politicians thus elected repaid them with suitable favours. "One hand washes the other," as the Italian saying has it. For the *mafiosi* it was a golden age. Soft-spoken bosses extorted whatever they wanted from the Sicilian economy and basked in respect.

The coming of Mussolini upset things for a while. The dictator could not countenance the challenge to his absolute power that the Mafia represented. Cesare Mori, the tough Prefect sent to Palermo with orders to clean up Sicily, spelt out the new policy with brutal frankness. "If the Sicilians are afraid of the *mafiosi*, I'll convince them that I am the most powerful *mafioso* of them all." For a time, it seemed that Mori had almost eliminated the Mafia, but the cure was short-lived. Many of the *mafiosi* had sought exile in the United States, and in 1943 they were able to return to Sicily on the coattails of the United States Army. The Americans had planned to use the gangsters as a weapon of war against Mussolini, but the plan had unforeseen

consequences. Mussolini's state vanished like a puff of smoke before the Allied onslaught: the returned *mafiosi*, however, thrived.

In some ways, the Mafia found life in Italy after World War II very difficult. Emigration—both within Italy and across its borders—took away much of the population the Mafia had previously battened on, and the massive development of the south left many of the old-style bosses reeling with the same sort of culture shock that afflicted their more law-abiding compatriots.

The Mafia did not die out, however. It changed. By the 1970s, it and its sister societies—the 'Ndrangheta of Calabria and the Camorra of Naples—had turned themselves into modern business enterprises, using criminal activities to finance more-or-less legitimate enterprises under their control. Among other things, they invested in enough heroin-producing equipment to provide an estimated 30 per cent of American consumption. Naturally, it made good business-sense to create a thriving home market for heroin, too: the Mafia has never allowed human misery to stand in its way.

The Mafia's transformation may in the long run prove to be its downfall. The old-style organization owed much of its strength to the essentially family loyalties on which it laid its foundations: the celebrated code of silence observed by its members, both in and out of police custody, was based on a perverted sense of honour as well as a straightforward fear of reprisal. Such loyalties are harder to engender in a Mafia in which computers and cost-accountants take pride of place over the old "men of respect" and, by offering immunities to informers, the Italian authorities have recently made head-

way against their oldest enemy. Nevertheless, according to a 1982 estimate, Italy's criminal economy—which is largely under Mafia control—was worth around 10 billion dollars. It is unlikely to disappear.

Whether the fabric of society can match the Mafia's resilience is a contentious question in Italy. Scorched by the forges of social change, seduced by consumerism and undermined by narcotics, in theory the Italian family should be approaching the status of an endangered species. Many Italians, in fact, are ready to declare the family extinct, even in the supposedly tradition-bound south.

"The old loyalties have disappeared," claims Luisa A. in Naples. "Everyone's out for himself. You even hear of people putting their parents into old folks' homes—we're as bad as the Milanese, now."

"Once upon a time," explains a Tuscan restaurateur, "the family meant something. Now? Italian civilization's a joke. A new car, a washing machine—that's all they care about. No wonder the kids are killing themselves with drugs." "The Italian family?" asks a Milanese intellectual. "You've been watching too many old films. We're just another Western European country now—a few years behind the rest, maybe, but on the same road."

Interestingly, though, it is usually other people's families who are considered to have died out. Luisa, for example, returned from a lengthy stint in Milan at least in part because she wanted to be with her ageing parents. The Tuscan's restaurant is entirely a family-run affair—and several times a week it is packed out with vast, deafeningly cheerful family parties. (They only get together for special occasions these days, most of them explain; but they manage to find plenty of occasions special enough to justify holding a re-union.) And most Milanese, despite what some southerners may claim, would think it quite shameful to send their old folk into institutions—supposing the Italian state were ever to provide enough of them.

The Italian family, in short, may not be the unshakeable foundation that it once was; but it has held out far better than its equivalents elsewhere. Indeed, not all of the changes have worked against the family. Traditionally, for instance, children lived at home with their parents until they were married. In the 1960s they were infected by Anglo-Saxon notions of breaking away, but today a chronic housing shortage is once more forcing children to stay at home until their wedding day, and sometimes even after it.

If Italians manage to hold on to their family way of life, they may be better placed than other nations to face the challenge of a rapidly changing future. The already dawning electronic age and the imminent information explosion promise to decentralize dramatically the means of wealth production. In such circumstances, Italy's lack of strong government could be an advantage, not a crippling defect, and all those resourceful, mutually supportive families could turn out to be a national asset that more disciplined nations will come to envy.

Italians living today have seen their country survive one dramatic transformation. If need be, they can survive another. They are not invulnerable to chaos and crisis, but they have learnt to live with them. They may yet have to teach the rest of Europe how it is done.

In Rome, a nun teaches council estate children a song *(top)*, **and a sister lends a supporting arm to an elderly woman on a stroll beside the Venetian lagoon** *(above)*. **All over Italy, the needy find a second family in the Church, which performs many social services.**

As if paying a social call on their departed relatives, families crowd a cemetery in southern Italy's Basilicata region on the Sunday after All Souls' Day, when the dead are remembered. On most Sundays, there are mourners who have come to address their thoughts to the deceased.

THE COMPANIONABLE SPIRIT OF SUNDAY

For the gregarious Italians, Sundays are above all else a time of sociability. Unlike nations for whom the day of rest means peace and quiet or the single-minded pursuit of a hobby, Italians at leisure consider that the greatest pleasure is to pass the time in the company of friends and relations. Family parties gather for lunch in seaside cafés or country *trattorie*, stretching the meal out for half the afternoon. Old men while away the hours round café tables. Young people flock together to flirt in groups that constantly dissolve and reform. Sometimes the entertainment is on a less intimate scale, because throughout the length and breadth of the peninsula Sunday is also the day for the nation's favourite mass spectator sport, football. The enthusiasts who crowd in to watch the matches enjoy taking part in the spectacle, with flamboyant demonstrations of support for local teams.

Such is their appetite for company that Italians can turn the most unpromising events into social occasions. A Sunday-morning visit to a cemetery, for instance, often takes on a neighbourly air as mourners address themselves to the other visitors—and sometimes also to the dead. Even traffic jams can provide a certain camaraderie: finding themselves in the company of other people and with time to kill, what else should the frustrated motorists do but hobnob?

Steadied by many hands, a supporter at a football match manipulates a heavy banner in an energetic exhibition of strength and skill.

Drivers in the summer weekend jam between Florence and the sea chat and stroll philosophically on the motorway.

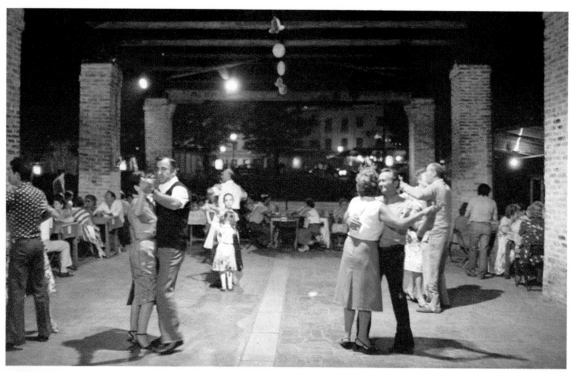

On a Sunday evening in the little riverside town of Dolo near Padua, a handful of couples of widely differing ages dance quietly on the stone terrace of a neighbourhood café. At the tables, families converse in the warm dusk.

Against a backdrop of empty deckchairs, members of a family linger over a midday picnic on a Rimini beach. Before noon and later in the day the beach is packed with family groups, but at lunchtime most retire to nearby restaurants.

Flocks of locals on the Venetian island of Pellestrina watch as a fisherman attempts a traditional feat of skill and daring. His aim is to make his way along a greased spar and reach the flag.

A relaxed group of young people idle away the afternoon in the piazza of Forte dei Marmi, a seaside resort in Tuscany that has become their customary Sunday meeting place. They come on their motorcycles and mopeds from all over the region to enjoy each other's company.

Outside a bar in Sacile, a small town in the north-east of Italy, elderly men sit over glasses of wine beneath signs offering sandwiches for sale. Their wives remain at home, preparing the Sunday meal.

2

A HISTORY OF DISUNITY

Italy became a political entity little more than a century ago. Between the collapse of the Roman Empire in the fifth century A.D. and the unification of Italy in 1861, no ruler had made himself master of the entire peninsula; indeed, none had even tried. Italy remained, as the Austrian statesman Metternich remarked in 1849, merely a "geographical expression".

Foreign powers dominated Italy for much of the period of disunity. But during the Middle Ages, scores of Italian towns governed themselves and their surrounding countryside with hardly any outside interference. The city-states developed strong local loyalties which remained a potent force even after unification. In the 20th century, the dictator Mussolini artificially fanned nationalism by harking back to the Roman Empire. Since World War II, remarkable economic progress has given Italians a new and genuine pride in their nation. But thanks to a fragmented history, local affections still find as large a space as national allegiance in most Italians' hearts.

Before the Romans engulfed it, the Italian peninsula was, in common with the rest of Europe, divided like a chequerboard between tribal groups representing a variety of ethnic strains. Some were of Mediterranean origin; others had moved across the Alps from central and northern Europe. By the eighth century B.C., they numbered among them two civilizations vastly more sophisticated than the rest—one and possibly both of them imported. The city-states of Greece had founded thriving colonies in Sicily and along the coast of southern Italy; and in central Italy the Etruscans had emerged as a vigorous and artistic trading people. The Etruscan language was quite different from those of the other tribes in Italy and, according to one theory, the people originated in Asia Minor.

At the time the Etruscans began to flourish in Italy, Rome was no more than a well-used ford near the mouth of the Tiber River. But in the sixth century B.C., Etruscan colonists subjugated the local people—the Latin tribes—and a great city was developed.

For almost a century, Etruscan kings ruled Rome and the surrounding towns and countryside. They gave their subjects their alphabet, derived from that of the Greeks, and many of their religious and cultural practices. But the city's language remained Latin. At the end of the sixth century B.C., the Latins overthrew their Etruscan kings, and the new Roman republic that established itself emerged as the natural leader of the city-states of Latium.

Over the next 200 years, republican Rome gained control of central Italy, absorbing its allies and destroying its enemies. In the south, the Greek colonists retained their autonomy as allies of Rome, but were later annexed. The republic's trump card was its army, which had the incalculable advantage

A detail from the continuous frieze of Trajan's Column shows Roman legionnaires presenting the Emperor with the severed heads of soldiers from vanquished Dacia—now Rumania. The marble monument was built in 113 A.D. to record Trajan's military career.

of organization against which enemies could muster only brute force and raw courage. The army's discipline was harsh. Cowards were flogged to death; disobedience by officers or men was punishable by beheading; thieves and deserters had their right hands cut off.

The basic Roman fighting unit, the legion, comprised 4,200 infantrymen, 300 cavalrymen and various supporting elements. The legion's backbone was the infantry, who were drawn up in three lines for their battles. The first line discharged short throwing spears, then rushed forwards to engage in hand-to-hand combat with short swords; if they failed to repel the enemy, the second line repeated the same sequence and the third line, armed with long spears, formed a reserve.

Pressing northwards in the third and second centuries B.C., the Romans established their hegemony as far as the southern slopes of the Alps. As its sway expanded, Rome produced a succession of superb civil engineers who knitted the republic's conquests together by means of a network of roads. Some of the earliest of these highways, made of polygonal blocks of tufa carefully fitted together on a bed of gravel, are still in existence and have withstood centuries of use.

The conquest of Italy presented few serious obstacles, but during the third century B.C. Rome fought two prolonged and costly wars against Carthage, the dominant sea power of the western Mediterranean. In the year 218 B.C., the great Carthaginian leader Hannibal managed to bring an army equipped with war elephants across the Mediterranean, through Spain and over the Alpine passes into Italy. Al-

though he devastated much of the open country, his forces proved to be no match for the rugged, indestructible Roman infantry, and Hannibal was forced to sue for peace.

The defeat of Carthage opened the way to still more extensive Roman conquests, from North Africa to England, and from Spain to Syria. The Mediterranean became a Roman lake—*mare nostrum*, our sea. There were Roman colonies along the Rhine and the Danube; Roman governors in Athens and Alexandria. At home, the city of Rome itself grew into a metropolis of more than a million inhabitants, and was known far and wide as *caput mundi*, the capital of the world.

Meanwhile, discontent was growing in the Italian countryside. One grievance voiced by the populace was that imports of foreign corn undermined

Archaeologists investigate the Roman
Forum foundations, continuing the
excavation which began in the 19th
century. Between the 6th century B.C.
and the 2nd century A.D., the Forum
evolved from a marketplace into the
ceremonial hub of the imperial empire.

Italian agriculture, another that the fortunes won in distant corners of the empire were creating a new gulf between rich and poor.

The first century B.C. was marked by civil war and insurrection, which the republican government was unable to contain. In 73 B.C. the Thracian slave Spartacus escaped with 70 others from a school for gladiators and quickly gathered an army of 70,000 runaway slaves, disaffected peasants and bandits. For two years Spartacus harried the countryside and outmanoeuvred the legions sent against him, until he was slain in the mountains of Calabria.

Two decades later, some of the generals of the Roman armies began plotting against the authority of the state. Julius Caesar, the brilliant strategist who had conquered Gaul—present-day France—revolted against the republic in 49 B.C., when he and one of his legions crossed the frontier into Italy in direct contravention of Roman law. After defeating his rival, Pompey, he crushed other insurgents in Asia Minor with his usual efficiency—a ruthless style made all the more impressive by the lapidary brevity of his dispatches from the field. *Veni, vidi, vici*—I came, I saw, I conquered—he wrote in the letter announcing the victory at Zela, where he defeated a Persian vassal. Soon after, he had himself declared dictator for life, but in 44 B.C. his career was cut short by the daggers of his enemies Brutus and Cassius.

After another struggle for power, Caesar was succeeded by his grand-nephew Octavian, who styled himself Caesar Augustus and established a new monarchical order, in which Rome and its possessions were ruled by an all-powerful emperor. His successors on the throne continued to be known as

A monumental bust of the Emperor Constantine, sculpted a few years before his death in 337 A.D., betrays the stern piety of a convert. Constantine, Rome's first Christian emperor, built churches, commissioned bibles and abolished crucifixion in the Empire.

Caesars. Though their despotism produced a predictable upsurge of internal corruption, the Empire itself continued to expand. By the second century of the Christian era, as Edward Gibbon remarks on the opening page of his marathon history, *The Decline and Fall of the Roman Empire*, the territory ruled by Rome "comprehended the fairest part of the earth, and the most civilized portion of mankind".

Never before had so many nations lived at peace with one another. From Libya to Britain and Gadix (Cadiz) to Armenia there was one official language, one codified body of civil and criminal law, one system of coinage, of weights and measures, of government administration, of reckoning time.

Although Rome set the style in most things, it also absorbed the myriad cultural influences provided by its diverse provinces. Greek teachers instructed the Romans in science, philosophy and literature; Greek sculptors furnished the prototypes of Roman statues.

At the same time, the influx of orientals into Rome created new standards of opulence and physical well-being. The public baths, or *thermae*, became the centre of social life—their walls covered with marble and mosaics, their waters flowing from silver taps into marble basins. Men of leisure spent all afternoon at the baths, lounging in the courtyards or listening to the poets and declaimers who recited in the lecture rooms; adjoining gymnasia had facilities for sports and ball games.

From the eastern provinces came mystery cults that supplemented and eventually supplanted the Roman state religion, with its pantheon headed by Jupiter, Juno and Minerva. These cults—promising the faithful life after death—helped to prepare the ground for the advent of Christianity, which reached Rome during the first century.

The early Christians were alternately tolerated and cruelly persecuted by the imperial authorities. For more than 200 years their church remained an underground movement. But early in the fourth century, the Emperor Constantine was converted to Christianity. In a series of edicts he declared the pagan religions to be mere *superstitio* and made Christianity the state religion of Rome, thus giving the church a new and unaccustomed role as one of the main supporting pillars of imperial policy.

Politically and militarily, however, the Empire was already in disarray. Barbarian armies from the north and east had overrun its outlying defences and had pillaged such cities as Antioch and Lugdunum (Lyons). Under this onslaught, the government was decentralized, since it was impossible for one ruler to control the widely scattered imperial armies. In 330, Constantine removed the seat of empire from Rome to Byzantium, on the Bosphorus, where he established a new capital city called

43

2

Constantinople. In 395, the Empire split into two units, each with its own emperor; Ravenna became the capital of the western section.

But the new arrangement failed to protect Italy. In the first decade of the fifth century, Rome was sacked by the armies of Alaric the Visigoth. When this invasion was followed by that of other Germanic tribes, notably the Huns, the end was a foregone conclusion. In 476, the last titular emperor of the West, a young boy named Romulus Augustulus, was deposed by the Danubian general Odoacer, who ruled for 13 years as the first barbarian king of Italy—nominally under the aegis of the Emperor of the East.

Although the Byzantine emperors made sporadic efforts to reassert their authority in Italy, their forces were no match for the various local powers that divided up the peninsula during the centuries that followed. Admittedly Sicily, captured by Byzantium in the sixth century, retained its allegiance to the Eastern Empire until the ninth century, and there were imperial officials in Calabria until the 11th century. But in the north, Teutonic invaders known as the Lombards established independent duchies, while in central Italy the popes—the bishops of Rome who were gradually becoming universally accepted as the spiritual leaders of Christendom—became temporal rulers.

The popes had acquired their territory by opposing Lombard expansion southwards into Byzantine territory. In a bid to contain their enemies, the popes called in assistance from the kings of the Franks (French), who by the eighth century had become the most powerful rulers north of the Alps. First Pepin and then his son Charle-magne descended into Italy and fought victorious campaigns. They handed the papacy the lands that the Lombards had wrested from Byzantium—a belt crossing Italy diagonally from Ravenna to Rome—and retained the territories to the north for themselves.

Meanwhile, Charlemagne had conquered or allied himself with all the tribes of Germany and forcibly baptized any who were pagan. For his achievement in unifying the greater part of western Christendom, he was crowned "Roman Emperor" by Pope Leo III at the altar of St. Peter's Basilica in Rome on Christmas Day, 800.

The alliance between the Pope and Charlemagne led to the establishment of the Holy Roman Empire—an empire that existed in theory rather than in practice, as the political expression of the medieval idea of a universal Christian monarchy. The pope was to be guardian of its spiritual values, and a temporal Caesar, drawn from the ranks of the northern kings, would act as defender of the faith. In name, at least, this shadowy empire survived for a thousand years. It served primarily as a mantle of legitimacy for the titular emperors of Germany and Austria, who inherited Charlemagne's epithet when his line died out. They reigned as Holy Roman Emperors until the title was abolished by Napoleon in 1806.

Whatever its implications for the rest of Europe, the Holy Roman Empire was to have far-reaching effects on subsequent Italian history. By granting the popes temporal power over central Italy, it served to cut off the north from the south, and thus divided the peninsula into three mutually suspicious zones. In addition, it linked the fate of Italy with that of Germany and Austria, providing an open door to foreign interference in Italian affairs.

Although the popes continued to crown the emperors, relations between the two powers deteriorated sharply after Charlemagne's reign: the ensuing centuries saw them locked in a bitter struggle for the control of Italy. The populace split into two parties, papalist and imperialist, which assumed the names of Guelph and Ghibelline respectively. Often one town would be torn by rivalry between the two sides.

But during the first part of the 12th century, a succession of emperors showed little interest in the affairs of Italy. Many cities took advantage of the lull in outside interference to usurp the imperial powers. By the end of the 12th century, large parts of Italy had become a mosaic of miniature republics, each consisting of a city and its surrounding countryside. The republics jealously guarded their autonomy after the emperors renewed their attentions. Even in areas with a monarchical style of government, such as the Papal States, cities enjoyed a good deal of independence. The communes proved fertile seedbeds for new ideas, artistic movements and commercial ventures.

In the early years of the independent city-states, government in theory rested with the whole body of the citizens; in practice, however, only the more prominent members of the community normally participated. Subsequently, personal rule by a strong man became more common, though the forms of a republic were often maintained. By the late 14th century, when both popes and emperors at last desisted from interfering in the communes' affairs, despotic dynasties had installed themselves almost everywhere.

The Tuscan city of Florence was one of the wealthiest of the communes. Wool was the source of its prosperity; the cloth woven there was known and sold throughout all of Europe. By the 14th century, Florence was a city of about 100,000 inhabitants, and had 110 churches, 39 monasteries and convents. There were more than 200 shops belonging to the wool merchants' guild, producing cloth valued annually at 1.2 million florins—the florin being a highly prized gold coin first minted in the republic in 1252.

The new money of the merchant class eventually eroded the powers of the old nobility. The government of the city, although nominally republican, was essentially an oligarchy administered by and for the rich merchants.

A CHRONOLOGY OF KEY EVENTS

c.1000 B.C. Iron-age culture spreads throughout the Italian peninsula, which is inhabited by many different tribes speaking diverse languages.

750–670 B.C. Greek city-states found colonies in Sicily and southern Italy. Phoenicians from Carthage colonize western Sicily and Sardinia.

750–600 B.C. The Etruscans develop a great civilization in Tuscany and Latium. They build cities, trade widely and display their artistry in sculptures of terra cotta (*above*) and bronze.

616–509 B.C. Etruscan kings rule Rome, a strategically placed city inhabited by a Latin-speaking people. Rome begins to dominate the surrounding towns.

509 B.C. The Romans overthrow their foreign rulers and set up a republic.

348–269 B.C. In stages, the Romans conquer or ally themselves with all the peoples of central and southern Italy.

264–238 B.C. The Romans wage the First Punic War against the Carthaginians. The victorious Romans annex Sicily, Sardinia and Corsica, the first of many overseas provinces.

218–201 B.C. The Carthaginian leader Hannibal initiates the Second Punic War by invading Italy via Gaul (present-day France) and the Alps. The Romans win, and take much of Spain from the Carthaginians.

58–44 B.C. The great Roman general Julius Caesar conquers Gaul. In a bid for power, Caesar returns to Italy with his army against the government's instructions. Civil war ensues. Caesar, victorious, becomes dictator in 47 B.C. Three years later, he is assassinated.

27 B.C.–14 A.D. Julius Caesar's adopted son Augustus (*above, being crowned by Victory*) reigns as Rome's first emperor. The whole Italian peninsula is incorporated into the Roman state. Rome now rules the entire Mediterranean world; the city is rebuilt with the appropriate grandeur.

40–100 Christianity spreads through the eastern part of the Empire and reaches Rome.

79 Vesuvius erupts; Pompeii (*below*) and Herculaneum are destroyed.

117 The Roman Empire reaches its greatest size, stretching from the Caspian to the Atlantic and from Britain to Egypt.

313–337 The Emperor Constantine makes Christianity the official religion of the Empire. The western part of the empire is in economic decline and Constantine builds a new capital, Constantinople, in the East.

381 The bishop of Rome claims pre-eminence over other Christian bishops and assumes the title "Papa"—father.

395 The Empire is split in two. Constantinople remains the capital of the Eastern Empire; Ravenna becomes the capital of the Western Empire.

395–476 Waves of invaders from northern and central Europe weaken the Western Empire. In 476 the barbarian chief Odoacer deposes the Western Roman Emperor and rules Italy in his stead.

c.529 Saint Benedict, a native of Umbria, formulates the rules which will govern monastic life in Western Europe.

535–555 Justinian, Emperor of the East, invades Italy and topples the barbarians from power. Italy becomes an outlying province of the Eastern Empire.

568 The Lombards, a Germanic people, enter Italy. In the next few years they conquer much of it. The Eastern Empire retains Sicily, the far south of the peninsula, and a band across Italy from Ravenna to Rome.

732–756 The Lombards encroach on Ravenna and Rome. Pope Stephen II invites Pepin, the King of France, to attack the Lombards. Pepin forces the Lombards out of their newly conquered territories; instead of returning these lands to the Eastern Empire, he gives them to the Pope. This marks the beginning of the Papal States.

774 Pepin's son Charlemagne defeats the Lombards and rules over their lands in Italy. He confirms the Pope's right to govern the band of territory between Ravenna and Rome.

800 Charlemagne, now ruler of much of Western Europe, is crowned Holy Roman Emperor by Pope Leo III.

827–878 Arabs conquer Sicily and the southern mainland. Under their rule, the area prospers and intellectual life flourishes.

1030–1137 Normans conquer Sicily and southern Italy, and establish an efficient rule.

1100–1200 Scores of northern cities, theoretically under the rule of the Holy Roman Emperor or the Eastern Emperor, become virtually self-governing.

1204–1472 Venice acquires a great overseas empire, which includes Crete, Cyprus and the Dalmatian coast.

1209 Saint Francis of Assisi (*below*) founds an order of mendicant friars.

1220–1250 Inheriting the Holy Roman Empire from his father, and Sicily with southern Italy from his Norman mother, Frederick II of Hohenstaufen reigns gloriously in the south but fails to impose his authority on the northern communes.

1266 A French prince, Charles of Anjou, takes over southern Italy and Sicily at the invitation of the Pope.

1271 Marco Polo embarks from Venice on a 24-year long journey through the Far East.

1282 In an uprising known as the "Sicilian Vespers", the Sicilians revolt against the French and bestow the crown of Sicily on the Spaniard Peter of Aragon.

1305 A French Pope, Clement V, transfers the seat of the Papacy to Avignon, where it will remain for 72 years.

1348 The bubonic plague kills one third of the population of Italy.

1434 Cosimo de' Medici (*above*) gains power in Florence. He and his successors patronize the artists and philosophers of the Renaissance.

1442 The French line ruling southern Italy dies out, and the Spanish king of Sicily wins control of the southern mainland.

1494 Charles VIII of France, pretender to the crown of southern Italy, invades the peninsula. Piero de' Medici, ruler of Florence, co-operates

1350–1454 During a century of warfare, the communes of Florence, Venice (*above*) and Milan swallow up other city-states. By 1454, when the Peace of Lodi is agreed, Italy consists of five major states and a few minor ones.

1360 The Tuscan-born poet Francesco Petrarca (Petrarch) publishes his lines addressed to Laura, an idealized beloved. In his aim—the enrichment of the human mind and conscience—he prefigures the Renaissance, and his verses will have a strong influence on European poetry for centuries.

with the enemy and is driven out of the city. The friar Savonarola sets up a short-lived republic in Florence. The French take southern Italy but by 1496 the Spaniards have driven them out.

1503 Julius II becomes Pope and makes Rome the centre of High Renaissance art and learning.

1525–1559 Spain gains control of most of northern Italy.

1545–1563 The Council of Trent, the key event in the Counter-Reformation, clarifies Catholic doctrine and decrees reforms in the clergy.

1613 Galileo, the first scientist to use a telescope (*below*), produces evidence that the earth revolves round the sun.

1713 Spain is weakened by war and most of her Italian possessions—notably Milan and the south—are acquired by Austria. Sicily is handed to the Duke of Savoy, ruler of French Savoy and Italian Piedmont.

1720 The Duke of Savoy exchanges Sicily for the Kingdom of Sardinia.

1734 Spain re-takes southern Italy and Sicily.

1796–1799 The French Revolutionary army, led by Napoleon, conquers Italy and sets up a number of republics modelled on the French one. An Austrian offensive and Nationalist risings force the French to withdraw from Italy by 1799.

1800–1814 Napoleon reconquers Italy. In 1805, he bestows on himself the crown of Italy (*right*); by 1809 the whole peninsula is ruled directly or indirectly from France. The French introduce a modern legal system and improve the administration.

1815 At the Congress of Vienna, held after Napoleon's downfall, Italy is

repartitioned among its former rulers. A branch of the Spanish Bourbon dynasty is reinstated in the south, the Pope retains the centre, Austria most of

the north, and the King of Sardinia Piedmont.

1832 The exiled revolutionary Giuseppe Mazzini (*above*) founds Young Italy, a movement for national unity.

1848 A popular uprising in Palermo spreads to other areas; in response, liberal constitutions are granted in several states, including Piedmont. While Austria has internal rebellions, Venice and Milan free themselves.

1849 Following unrest in Rome and the flight of the Pope, a republic is founded. The republican army, led by Giuseppe Garibaldi, is defeated by French forces, and the Pope returns. Rebellions in other states are crushed by Austria, and the new constitutions repealed everywhere except in Piedmont.

1859 Camillo Cavour, Prime Minister of Piedmont, makes a treaty with France to rid Italy of the Austrians.

1859 France defeats the Austrians at Magenta and Solferino. Austria loses Lombardy to the French, who cede it to Piedmont. The rulers of Parma, Modena and Tuscany—all Austrian satellite princes—flee Italy.

1860 In plebiscites held in Parma, Modena and Tuscany, the populations vote for unity with Piedmont. Revolutionaries in Sicily request Garibaldi's help. He embarks from Genoa with 1,100 volunteers. Garibaldi quickly takes Sicily in the name of Victor Emmanuel, the King of Sardinia and ruler of Piedmont, then crosses to the mainland. As he approaches Naples, the capital of the southern realm, its ruler flees. Meanwhile the regular Piedmontese army annexes the Papal States. Italy is now almost united but the Pope, supported by the French, retains Rome and its environs, and Austria keeps the north-east.

1861 Victor Emmanuel (*above*) becomes king of Italy. The constitution of Piedmont is used for the new nation, and Turin becomes the capital.

1866 After a war with Austria, Italy acquires the state of Venice.

1870 France, occupied with the Franco-Prussian War, withdraws troops from Rome. The Italian army marches on Rome and the Pope surrenders. He is granted sovereignty over the Vatican City but refuses to recognize the new order. Rome becomes the seat of national government.

1870–1914 More than 10 million Italians emigrate—mainly to other European countries, Brazil, Argentina and the United States.

1887–1896 Italy attempts to conquer Ethiopia, but is driven out.

1896–1900 Socialist agitators promote disorder among Italians restive because of harvest failures and unemployment. Military rule is imposed in some areas.

1899 Giovanni Agnelli founds the car manufacturing company Fiat.

1909 Guglielmo Marconi, inventor of the wireless, receives a Nobel prize.

1912 Italy takes Libya from Turkey.

1914–1918 World War I breaks out. After Britain and France agree to back Italy's claims to the Trentino, the Alto Adige, Trieste and northern Dalmatia, Italy declares war on Austria in 1915 and on Germany in 1916. Italy suffers several defeats but in the final months of war makes a notable contribution to the Allied victory.

1919–1921 The peace treaty of World War I grants Italy the Trentino, the

Alto Adige and Trieste. However, Dalmatia becomes part of Yugoslavia and Fiume, an Italian-speaking city on the Croatian coast, becomes a Free Port. The poet Gabriele d'Annunzio at the head of a band of fanatics seizes control of Fiume and rules the city for more than a year.

1919–1921 Amid social and economic turbulence and discontent over the outcome of the war, Benito Mussolini forms bands of thugs known as *fasci di combattenti*. A weak coalition government stands back while the Fascists destroy headquarters of the Socialist and Communist parties and break strikes.

1921 Mussolini and 34 other Fascists are elected to Parliament.

1922 After breaking a general strike, the Fascists seize key communication points, threatening to isolate Rome from the rest of the country. Victor Emmanuel III invites Mussolini to form a government.

1923 Mussolini devises a new electoral system which will ensure a huge Fascist majority, and parliament accepts it.

1925–1926 Mussolini begins to rule openly as dictator.

1929 Mussolini concludes the Lateran Treaty with the Papacy (*above*). The Pope at last recognizes the Kingdom of Italy; Catholicism is confirmed as the state religion.

1935 Italy attacks Ethiopia and in 1936 proclaims an Italian empire.

1936–1939 Italy and Germany support General Franco in the Spanish Civil War.

1939 Mussolini and Hitler sign a military treaty, the Pact of Steel. World War II breaks out.

1940 Italy declares war on France and Britain.

1943 British and American armies land in Sicily. The Fascist regime collapses and Mussolini is arrested. In the south, where the Allies quickly gain control, a new Italian government declares war on Germany. Mussolini, freed by German commandos, establishes a rival government in the north.

1945 Mussolini is captured and shot by partisans. World War II ends.

1946 A popular referendum abolishes the monarchy.

1945–1953 Alcide de Gasperi, the leader of the Christian Democrat Party, heads seven successive administrations.

1947 A new republican constitution is approved.

1950–1970 Italy industrializes rapidly, to become one of the seven largest economies in the world.

1978 Former prime minister Aldo Moro is kidnapped and murdered by the Red Brigades. This is the culmination of several years of attacks on citizens by left and right-wing terrorists.

1981 Giovanni Spadolini, leader of the Republican Party, becomes the first non-Christian Democrat Prime Minister since 1945.

2

The masters of the guilds regulated every detail of trade.

The wealth of Florence gave it an educated leisure class that tended to disperse its energies in political feuds between the Guelph and Ghibelline parties. The Ghibellines were eventually expelled and the Guelphs split into two factions, the Whites and the Blacks. But the élite also produced the first stirrings of the humanism that was to blossom into the Italian Renaissance, the revival of classical science and philosophy, and of pagan themes in painting and sculpture. Dante Alighieri, the greatest Italian poet, was born in Florence in 1265 and had a thorough education in the Latin classics. The humanist scholar Leonardo Bruni wrote a century later, "by study of philosophy, theology, astrology, arithmetic and geometry, by reading history, by the turning over of many curious books, watching and sweating in his studies, he acquired the science which he was to adorn and explain in his verses."

Early in the 14th century, after the triumph of the Blacks over the Whites, Dante was banished from his native city with 600 others of the White party. He was never again to see the towers of Florence: instead, he spent the rest of his life wandering from one northern city to the next, seeking the protection of such patrons as the ruler of Verona, Can Grande della Scala, to whom he dedicated the *Paradiso* section of his greatest work, the *Divine Comedy*. Dante's *Commedia*—the adjective *Divina* was added to the title by a 16th-century editor—includes brilliant passages of documentary reporting as well as complex religious allegories, all expressed in resonant, melodic verse.

Dante died in Ravenna in 1321 after undertaking a diplomatic mission to Venice on behalf of the local ruler, Guido da Polenta. By then Ravenna had lost its erstwhile importance as the seat of emperors; the principal city-state on the Adriatic coast was Venice—no more than a collection of fishermen's huts under the Romans, but now grown wealthy and impregnable, thanks to the vast fleet of cargo vessels and fighting galleys with which it dominated the eastern Mediterranean.

During the 13th century, Venice had despoiled the Byzantine empire of many Greek islands and of extensive territory along the coasts of the Adriatic and the Black Sea. A long and bitter rivalry with the maritime republic of Genoa came to a head in 1379, when the Genoese sent a fleet to blockade the Venetians in their own lagoon—only to be caught in a trap at Chioggia, on the southernmost edge of the lagoon, where the flower of the Genoese navy was forced to surrender. Genoa never recovered from this crushing defeat, and Venice was left with uncontested mastery of the Mediterranean.

Venice, like Genoa, was a republic, but one of a curious sort. As the English writer James Morris put it, "Venice was a sort of police state, except that instead of worshipping power, she was terrified of it and refused it to any single one of her citizens." The governing body, the Council of Ten, controlled security agencies prepared to murder or imprison in order to prevent popular uprisings or personal dictatorship. The Doge, or chief magistrate, though able to assume real powers in times of emergency, was otherwise a figurehead. Usually the choice fell on someone past his prime, who was kept almost as a prisoner within his glorious palace. In a great water festival held each year on Ascension Day, the Doge would be rowed out to the mouth of the lagoon in his golden state barge and there, after the sea had been blessed with holy water, he would throw in a ring and pronounce the time-hallowed formula, "In sign of eternal dominion, we, the Doge of Venice, marry you, O sea!"

In the early 15th century, Venice consolidated its power by annexing the adjoining mainland states, including Padua, Vicenza and Verona. Soon afterwards the Venetians came into conflict with the dukes of Milan, who fought several bloody wars to prevent the republic of Venice from extending its frontiers into Lombardy.

This fertile, prosperous region had seen the establishment of some of the first European prototype banks in the 12th century; financiers from the city of Piacenza became so dominant in their profession that in northern Europe bankers and money lenders were known generically as "lombards". By the 14th century, Milan had become the foremost of the Lombard city-states. It proclaimed its affluence by erecting a series of churches and palaces that were larger and more splendid than anyone else's. The cathedral of Milan, begun in 1386, was designed to be the largest in the world, with capacity for 40,000 worshippers.

While the northern city-states competed and skirmished, the south was subjected to repeated invasions. Arabs conquered Sicily in the ninth century and then used the island as a base for expansion along the southern Italian coastline; Normans followed them two centuries later. Next it was the turn of the Hohenstaufen dynasty of south Germany and subsequently of the Angevins of south-western France. By the 15th century, the Spanish kings of Aragon were in control of Sicily and the southern mainland, which now was known as the Kingdom of Naples.

The 15th century was a period of consolidation everywhere in Italy. Powerful city-states swallowed up the weaker ones, and by the mid-century the great bulk of Italy fell within one of five states: Milan, Venice, Florence, the Papal States and the southern kingdom. Venice remained a republic, but Milan was by now a duchy ruled by the Sforza family, and Florence's affairs were directed by the Medici dynasty. The popes set about centralizing the government of their territory and became increasingly important temporal rulers. The office of supreme pontiff came to be regarded as an exclusively Italian preserve. Between the mid-15th century and the late 20th century, only three non-Italians were elected to the Holy See by the College of Cardinals. Many of the most famous landmarks of Renaissance Rome were built by worldly pontiffs of great taste and magnificence, belonging to one or another of the great Italian families, such as the Medici, the Farnese and the Rovere.

In the 16th century, the papacy was increasingly beset by a revolt in the Christian ranks—the Protestant Reformation. To counteract the growing power of the Protestants in Germany, England, the Netherlands and Scandinavia, successive popes carried out a wide-ranging programme of renewal, the Counter-Reformation. Outward symbols of this policy included the refurbishment of Rome under Pope Sixtus V in the 1580s, when the Lateran Palace was restored, many streets and squares rebuilt, dozens of monuments erected—and the great basilica of St. Peter's received its dome. Sixtus's administrative reforms were equally thorough. In only five years as pontiff, as one historian of the papacy expressed it, the indefatigable Sixtus "laid the foundations of that wonderful and silent engine of universal government by which Rome still rules the Catholics of every land on the face of the globe".

The period of the Church's triumph saw the decline of Italy's independent states as one after another fell under foreign domination. The foretaste of events to follow came in 1494 when Charles VIII of France, claiming lordship over Naples and Milan, invaded Italy from the north. His campaign proved to be a failure, but the ease with which he was expelled lulled Italian rulers into a false sense of security. It became their habit to invite in foreign powers to further their own political interests and, once entrenched, the allies proved impossible to oust. In the course of the 16th century, France did acquire some Italian territories but was driven out by Spain. Until the 18th century, the Habsburg kings of Spain ruled large parts of Italy and maintained a protectorate over most of the rest. Venice and the Papal States were the only substantial Italian territories to retain their independence. Spanish rule encouraged corruption and also damped initiative in a people already exhausted by war.

The death of the last Spanish Habsburg in 1700 resulted in conflict on a

A crowned figure of the Church triumphant dominates a painting of the Council of Trent, the 16th-century conference of bishops that launched the Counter-Reformation. The Council promoted ecclesiastical reforms and clarified disputed points of doctrine.

A CHARISMATIC PATRIOT

Giuseppe Garibaldi, the romantic hero of the Italian unification movement, was born in 1807 in Nice, which became part of Piedmont when he was seven. A passionate idealist, at 26 he met some of the men close to Giuseppe Mazzini, the exiled theorist behind the Risorgimento, and vowed to make his contribution to Italian unity. Soon afterwards, he took part in an unsuccessful republican plot against the Piedmont dynasty and was forced to flee to South America.

In exile, Garibaldi acquired formidable military skills—first as a sea captain, then as a guerrilla leader fighting for any cause he considered just. In that unruly continent, where every man was a law unto himself, Garibaldi inspired his troops by the sheer force of his personality—his courage, honesty and simplicity.

In 1848, Garibaldi returned to Italy to fight for its redemption. Twelve years later, he embarked on the military expedition for which he will always be remembered. Setting sail from Genoa with a band of 1,100 volunteers, he liberated Sicily and the southern mainland from their despotic ruler—uniting northern Italy with the south. The Italians elevated Garibaldi to the status of a saint and, when he was injured, scraps of his bloodstained clothing were treasured like holy relics. After his death in 1882, this one-time revolutionary was given a state funeral and mourned as a national hero.

A contemporary painting (*right, above*) **shows Garibaldi landing in Sicily in 1860 with the banner that became the flag of united Italy. The country's disunity is satirized by an 1866 cartoon** (*right*): **figures representing the northern regions strive to join hands with the south across the Papal States.**

European scale: the War of the Spanish Succession ended in 1713 with a young Bourbon king, a grandson of Louis XIV of France, enthroned in Madrid. In the interest of maintaining the balance of power in Europe between the Bourbons and the Habsburgs of Austria, Italy was carved up afresh. Most of the Spanish possessions passed to the Austrian Habsburgs—who were, on the whole, more enlightened and progressive rulers than the Spaniards had been. They streamlined the administration and developed the economy of territories under their control. However, the reforms were limited in scope and the Austrian overlords' minds were generally on matters other than Italy.

A minor beneficiary from the redistribution was Piedmont—a small independent buffer state between France and Milan—which gained Sicily. Such were the chess-game politics of the time that five years later the great powers obliged Piedmont's ruler to exchange Sicily for Sardinia. Not long afterwards, the Spanish Bourbons occupied Sicily and the southern mainland.

With roughly 300,000 inhabitants, the city of Naples, the capital of their realm, was then the second most populous city in Europe, after Paris. Under the Bourbons it became famed for the sumptuousness of its immense royal palace and its opera house, as well as for the squalor of its back streets. The monarchy's richest agricultural land was owned by the king, the nobles and the church. "If we divide all the families in the kingdom into sixty parts," wrote the priest and economics lecturer Abbé Antonio Genovesi in the 1760s, "one of these owns land and fifty-nine have not sufficient to be buried in."

The French Revolution, which set out to redress such inequities, launched

A painting portrays the carnage at Dogali, in Eritrea, where natives killed 500 Italian troops in 1887. Premier Francesco Crispi annexed Eritrea soon afterwards, but the slaughter was the first of many clashes that doomed Italy's empire-building in East Africa.

Italy on a fresh round of wars and massacres. In 1796, a republican army under General Napoleon Bonaparte invaded Italy and drove the Austrians out of the north. In the wake of his victorious campaign, Napoleon left a string of hastily formed Italian republics based on the French model. Ironically, the one existing republic, Venice, was abolished by a Napoleonic stroke of the pen and handed over to Austria as part of a peace package.

Napoleon soon became embroiled in Egypt; with French troops unavailable to defend their new sphere of influence in Italy, retribution was swift and ruthless. In 1799, throughout the peninsula the despots returned to their thrones and wreaked vengeance on the republicans. In the city of Naples, hundreds of supporters of the short-lived republic—mainly the young nobles and the city's intelligentsia—surrendered their arms to a monarchist army and an English fleet under Admiral Horatio Nelson, on condition that they would be allowed to sail to France or return to their homes unmolested. Instead, they were condemned to mass execution or life imprisonment as galley slaves.

With Napoleon's return to Europe, the pendulum swung once more in the other direction. In 1800, Napoleon, now France's First Consul, organized a new Italian campaign. By 1810, as Emperor of France, he controlled, directly or indirectly, the entire Italian peninsula: Piedmont, Tuscany and Rome were annexed to France; Venice and Milan formed the core of the Kingdom of Italy, ruled by Napoleon; and he installed his brother-in-law, Joachim Murat, as King of Naples.

In a decade or so of Napoleonic administration, many parts of Italy experienced their first taste of reasonably impartial, efficient government. Napoleon's officials brought energy and enthusiasm to provinces that had been demoralized by centuries of suffocating rule by foreign viceroys: they modernized the legal system, built new roads, bridges and schools, and trained regiments of soldiers in the latest fighting tactics. Moreover, because the French chose to ignore the old state boundaries, the inhabitants of the peninsula were encouraged to think of themselves as Italians rather than as Tuscans, Lombards, or whatever.

Napoleon's empire collapsed in 1814; the French withdrew from Italy and the absolutist regimes were reimposed at bayonet point. Their brutality and corruption made many people look back on the French occupation as a period of comparative freedom.

Thenceforth, the idea of Italian unity and independence increasingly attracted support among intellectuals, army officers, bureaucrats and a few nobles. A secret society known as the *Carboneria*—the charcoal-burners from whom it took its name spent much time working unseen in inaccessible forests—agitated for reforms in Naples and fomented revolutions in Parma, Modena and the Romagna, which were suppressed by force of Austrian arms.

When uncovered, members of the Carboneria were tortured, imprisoned and executed, but their fate failed to stamp out the freedom movement: Italian writers and composers began to engage in creating a subversive literature and even covertly nationalist operas that slipped through

2

the tight net of Austrian censorship. For example, in Giuseppe Verdi's 1842 opera *Nabucco*—Nebuchadnezzar—he portrayed the Jews of the Old Testament in captivity in Babylon. He conveyed their longing for deliverance in a moving chorus which the Italian public interpreted as their own prayer for liberation from the Austrian yoke. Giuseppe Mazzini, author of important works on Italian liberty and unity, spent most of his life in exile, rallying support for revolution.

In 1848, a year of unrest throughout all of Europe, Milan rose in revolt. The troops of Piedmont—which alone among the north Italian states was independent of Austria—came to the defence of Milan's provisional government in what came to be known as the First War of Independence. After four months, the war ended in defeat for Piedmont. The Venetians tried to throw off Austrian rule at the same time, but were starved into surrender after a five-month siege. In Rome, revolutionaries declared a republic that accomplished much for the city's poor but alienated the church and the wealthier citizens. Pope Pius IX left the Quirinal Palace disguised as a simple priest and fled to Neapolitan territory, whence he appealed to the French for aid. Allied with Austria, Naples and Spain, France moved quickly to crush an army of 10,000 Roman volunteers led by the self-taught guerrilla fighter Giuseppe Garibaldi.

Despite Garibaldi's defeat, the Italian Risorgimento, or resurgence, acquired what became an irresistible momentum. The Prime Minister of Piedmont and principal architect of Italian unification, Count Cavour, carefully orchestrated a new attack on Austria. This time a treaty with Napo-

leon III of France secured him as his ally. In 1859, the French won two major victories against the Austrians in northern Italy, at Magenta and Solferino, and forced them to agree to an armistice. Napoleon III's aim had been to secure Savoy and Nice for France; once these objectives were attained, he left Piedmont to its own devices.

While Cavour's agents annexed Tuscany and Emilia to Piedmont by means of hastily organized plebiscites, Garibaldi mustered a force of 1,100 volunteers—known as "The Thousand"—to go to the aid of the Sicilians, who had revolted against Francis II of Naples but were on the point of being crushed by a Neapolitan army of 20,000. Garibaldi landed at Marsala in Sicily in May 1860, fought a campaign of surprise and deception against the army of occupation, and soon had the entire island firmly in his grasp. In mid-August his irregulars crossed to the mainland and marched northwards. Three weeks later, Francis II fled from Naples only a day before Garibaldi entered the city and found himself greeted as a liberator by cheering crowds.

The Piedmontese reacted by sending a royal army marching south through the Papal States, and defeated a thin screen of papal troops at Castelfidardo. At Teano, north of Naples, Garibaldi's forces linked up with the army headed by Victor Emmanuel, the ruler of Piedmont, who was proclaimed king of a united Italy in March 1861. His capital, Turin, became the first capital of the whole country.

Only Venice and the rump of the Papal States still remained outside the borders of the new kingdom, the former to be ceded by Austria in 1866, the latter to be annexed in 1870, when the Italian army entered Rome following the

withdrawal of the city's French garrison. A plebiscite confirmed the Romans' overwhelming support for unity with Italy. At last the nation could move its seat of government to the city that was its logical capital.

One cloud hanging over united Italy was the implacable hostility of the Pope, shorn of almost all his temporal powers. A law was passed recognizing the Pope as an independent sovereign within the Vatican, the enclave of Rome encompassing St. Peter's and the headquarters of the Catholic Church. But Pius IX persisted in regarding himself as "the prisoner of the Vatican". He refused to treat with the new government and imposed a ban designed to prevent practising Catholics from voting in parliamentary elections.

There were additional reasons for the people of Italy to be less than fully committed to the new state. The regime was a constitutional monarchy with freedom of the press and without a secret police, but it had a highly centralized structure modelled on that of France, which was manifestly inappropriate for a nation with strong regional loyalties. Its constitution debarred illiterates from voting—not too serious an obstacle for Italians in the north, but for the south a barrier that disenfranchised more than 80 per cent of the voting-age population. Understandably, peasants and working men felt that they had no stake in the government; the south had exchanged an inefficient feudal government by Spanish agents for an unresponsive government by north-Italian bureaucrats, who understood it no better.

The first decades of Italian unity failed to achieve any dramatic gains internally, and successive governments

MUSSOLINI: THE PERFORMER

Mussolini wears the stony mask he assumed when listening to parliamentary speeches.

The dictator wields a shovel in a propaganda exercise to show him as a man of the people.

"I made my own rules and I did not keep even them," declared Benito Mussolini, and that cynical boast could serve as an epitaph for a man who was less a statesman than an actor—an exhibitionist who changed his role hourly to suit the occasion.

Born in 1883, the son of a socialist blacksmith and a devout Catholic schoolteacher, he was expelled from one school and suspended from another for stabbing fellow pupils. He subsequently completed his education but showed no intellectual sparkle. Between 1902 and 1919 he was by turns a teacher, bohemian, socialist agitator, soldier and journalist before he launched the fascist movement and promoted it through his newspaper.

After he became dictator of Italy in the mid-1920s, he devoted all his energy to the quest for adulation, using his propaganda machine to convince the people that he was, in his words, "the greatest personality in Europe". Boasting that he worked a 19-hour day running the state practically single-handed, he left his study lights burning while he took his habitual nine hours of sleep. Parliament survived only as a theatre for his spellbinding oratory, and reports of debates were sometimes doctored according to the requirements of publicity. Obsessed by physical prowess, he was always willing to show off his manly jaw and barrel chest for photographers, and at public meetings he concealed his shortness by standing on a stool. To demonstrate his vigour, he took to reviewing military parades at a run, a comic-opera effect heightened by the extravagant uniforms he affected.

Although Mussolini was well aware of Italy's military limitations, his envy of Hitler's conquests drove him to emulate the man he had once dismissed as a "silly little clown". After his downfall in 1943, he spent much of his last two years "thinking only of history and how he would appear in it".

2

tried to foster a sense of national purpose by means of foreign adventures. In the 1880s and 1890s, there were attempts to establish an imperial presence in Ethiopia—which ended in crushing defeat. Italy entered World War I on the side of the Allies in 1915 in the hope of acquiring Italian-speaking territories in Austria and of obtaining concessions in Africa, the Middle East and the eastern Mediterranean, where the Turkish empire was on the point of collapse. In a secret agreement signed in 1915, Britain and France agreed to almost all Italy's territorial demands. But the war proved far more costly than anyone had anticipated: Italy mobilized 5.2 million men, of whom nearly 700,000 lost their lives in a long, bloody stalemate on the Austrian front. At the peace table, Italy received large Austrian territories but failed to obtain the other territories it aspired to in Africa and the Balkans.

Disillusioned and impoverished, post-war Italy was ripe for new kinds of political adventurism. For 16 months in 1919 and 1920, the swashbuckling poet Gabriele d'Annunzio and a band of rag-tag followers occupied the port of Fiume, in Croatia, whose largely Italian population was fearful of being absorbed into newly created Yugoslavia.

D'Annunzio's posturings and pretensions served as an example to Benito Mussolini, a spellbinding orator who organized the black-shirted Fascist movement of the right as a counterweight to the rising influence of the Communists on the left of the political spectrum. Many of the *Fascisti* were street toughs with war experience, hostile to intellectuals and revolutionary workers, but not averse to political upheaval. Mussolini attracted them with a vague, patriotic philosophy: he professed to be on the side of the little man, of social reform and national awakening—a mixture of platitudes that had not been tried elsewhere in Europe, and had not earned the deserved opprobrium it has since gained.

When the Italian Socialists called a general strike in August 1922, the Fascists used the threat to public order as a pretext for seizing control of the public transport and communications systems, and were soon running the essential services themselves. At the end of October, their battalions threatened to enter Rome. Mussolini—now leader of the 35 Fascist deputies in Parliament—hurried from Milan and was appointed Premier by a thoroughly intimidated King Victor Emmanuel III.

Within three years, Mussolini had effectively short-circuited parliamentary democracy and had also assumed dictatorial powers. All opposition was silenced, by force if necessary. In 1924, the young Socialist leader Giacomo Matteotti, who had tried to have the recent election results declared invalid, was kidnapped and stabbed to death. Mussolini denied any association with the crime, but it was clear that the murderers were carrying out his wishes. Beginning with such arbitrary acts of violence, the Fascists soon succeeded in turning Italy into a well-organized police state. Political opponents of the regime were imprisoned or murdered, and civil rights were suppressed.

Initially, Mussolini had no coherent political programme and considered it an advantage—there would be fewer reasons for any opposition. Later he introduced a planned economy and involved the state in all aspects of life, from education and sport to commerce and industry. In 1929, his government negotiated the Lateran Treaty with the Vatican. The Catholic Church—for a large sum of money and acknowledgement as the official religion—at last recognized the Italian state.

The new *Duce* (leader) of Italy made earnest attempts to unite the population by such means as the prohibition of regional dialects and the standardization of the school curriculum. A vast propaganda machine glossed over the regime's crimes and errors, and whipped up popular enthusiasm for its achievements, including a clampdown on the Sicilian Mafia, the draining of the malaria-ridden Pontine marshes near Rome and—the feat most often quoted by foreigners—"making the trains run on time". In 1935, Europe watched with alarm and amazement when Mussolini sent an Italian expeditionary force to Ethiopia: its poison gas and machine guns made short work of an Ethiopian militia armed with spears and shotguns. It was said that Mussolini had revived the glories of the Roman Empire: wherever he put in an appearance, he was greeted by ecstatic crowds chanting *"Du-ce! Du-ce!"*.

But Mussolini's Ethiopian adventure served to estrange him from Britain and France, and propelled him into the orbit of Europe's other leading dictator, Adolf Hitler. The "Rome–Berlin Axis" established in 1936 fatally entangled Italian imperialism with the far more virulent belligerence of Nazi Germany. In June 1940, Mussolini led his country into World War II on the side of Germany and divided public opinion as never before. Three million Italians were conscripted into the armed forces to fight, often reluctantly, on the German side.

By 1943, the Axis had clearly outlived its usefulness; Hitler's armies had reached their high-water mark and were in retreat in Russia and North Africa, where their Italian allies had been forced to share their defeat. That summer, the British and American forces landed in Sicily. In July, while the Allies overran Sicily, dissident Fascists supported by the King and the High Command deposed the Duce. In September, the King and the army asked for an armistice; later the provisional government reversed alliances and declared war on Germany. Hitler's forces, however, rescued Mussolini, reinforced their defensive positions and set up a puppet regime in the north, the "Italian Social Republic". After a long campaign in which Italian partisans played a considerable role, the Germans finally surrendered in the spring of 1945. Mussolini was captured and killed by partisans when he tried to escape with the fleeing Germans.

The Italian monarchy had been discredited by its acceptance, albeit reluctant, of the Fascist dictatorship. In a referendum held in June 1946, 12.7 million Italians voted for a republic, as against 10.7 million who preferred the monarchist status quo. The royal family went into exile and the Republic of Italy was declared. In 1947, a new constitution was adopted. Italy became a member of the North Atlantic Treaty Organization (NATO) in 1949 and was a founder member of the European Economic Community (EEC) when it was established in 1957.

Even before the war was over, Italy had learnt its lesson from the catastrophic failure of authoritarianism. Back in the democratic mainstream, and freed from Mussolini's absurdly wasteful imperialism, post-war Italy quickly caught up with levels of culture and rates of economic advance that prevailed elsewhere in Europe. Success bred new confidence and optimism within the country, and enhanced its standing abroad. Once more the nation took its place as a highly respected member of the world community.

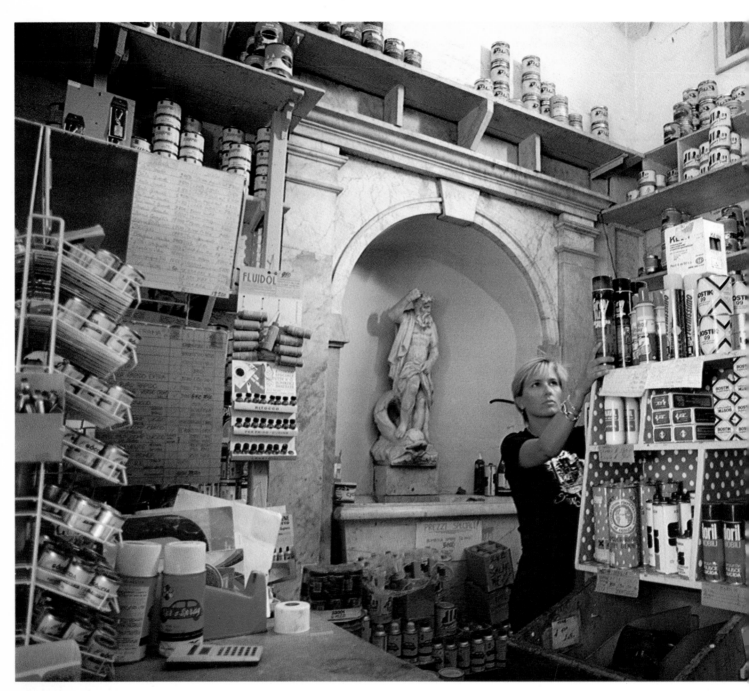

Cans of paint and aerosol sprays
surround a marble niche and sculpture
in an 18th-century Carrara mansion
that has become a hardware shop. As
the town's most plentiful raw material,
marble is used in buildings both
luxurious and simple, providing
everything from flooring to table tops.

58

CARRARA: MARBLE CAPITAL OF THE WORLD

For two thousand years, the men of Carrara have cut the world's most precious white stone from the Apuan Alps, peaks of solid marble that encircle the Tuscan town. The original quarry provided a gleaming cladding for the monuments of Imperial Rome. Renaissance sculptors prized Carrara's product for its snowy purity and compact grain; Michelangelo climbed the rock walls around the town many times in search of flawless pieces. Today, Carrara's river runs white with dust from around a million tonnes of marble cut annually, most of it destined to become architectural slabs or tombstones.

The marble workers of Carrara and the surrounding towns have handed down their skills over the generations. With the precision of diamond cutters, the quarriers split massive slabs away from the rockface. In the sawmills where the stone is cut and polished, craftsmanship is so fine that countries as distant as Brazil and India ship over rough marble for finishing to Italian standards. Sculptors around the world send small models to local artisans, who render them full-scale in marble. The traditions seem set to continue, for enough marble to last another millennium lies waiting in the hills.

Around the Carrara quarries, marble debris whitens the slopes like a snowfall. The bends in the mountain roads are so sharp that the lorries which haul the stone can negotiate them only by travelling in reverse gear on alternate zigs and zags.

Swallowed up in the vast mouth of a marble tunnel, a bulldozer waits to move blocks cut from a deep vein. Although the open rockface provides much of the quarries' stone, some fine deposits can be reached only by burrowing into the mountainside.

Balanced on scaffolding wedged into the sheer rockface, workmen cut plugs from the mountainside high above the quarry floor. The deep holes they leave will hold explosives that blast away the surface stone to expose the top-quality marble. The surface fragments are left scattered over the hillside.

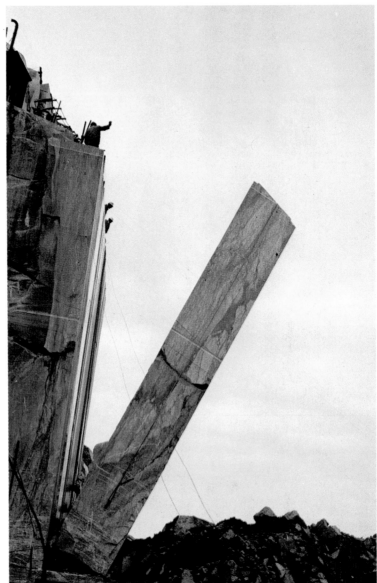

Severed from the mountainside with
the aid of hydraulic pulleys, a huge
marble block topples towards a bed of
rocky rubble, laid to serve as a cushion
for its fall. The stone sometimes breaks
on impact, but the huge fragments are
generally still large enough for use.

Rock-slicing cables festoon a stepped
quarry whose dark-veined marble is
unusual in an area famous for its white
stone. Pulleys work the cables against
an abrasive mixture of sand and water
that gradually carves the mountain's
jagged profile into neat blocks.

Wearing the paper hat traditionally worn by Carrara's stone workers to keep dust and debris out of their hair, an artisan models the back of a copy of the celebrated Greek sculpture Laocoon. The studio is crowded with reproductions destined to adorn public buildings round the world.

A craftsman roughs out a piece of modern sculpture with an electric drill. He has placed the sculptor's small-scale plaster model in front of him; several sets of callipers will help him transfer its exact proportions to the final, marble version.

In Carrara's main square, young artists
from around the world labour at
entries for the town's annual sculpture
contest. Competing by invitation, they
have two weeks to finish their works,
which later go on permanent display
along the local coastline.

A rare snowfall blankets vineyards on a high plateau in central Sicily. Although droughts and flash floods challenge farmers, the island is Italy's most productive wine region after Puglia. Its grapes are used for the fortified Marsala as well as for full-bodied table wines.

AN EXACTING LAND

Italy is a harsh land, for all its beauty, and in the days when the land itself was the people's only resource, few of them ever managed an easy living from it. Although the broad valley of the Po River, stretching across northern Italy, contains some of the most productive agricultural land in Europe, four fifths of the country's familiar form—that ragged boot, swinging down from its icy Alpine thigh to aim a never-quite-delivered kick at arid and unruly Sicily—is made up of mountains and hills. Those that do not defy farmers altogether are often too precipitous to be cultivated with machines. Erosion has stripped away much of the arable soil, especially in the south. Generations of grazing goats are partly to blame, but since Roman times humans have been equally responsible for the wasting of a once fertile landscape by burning trees to clear land and chopping them down for fuel and timber.

The climate, too, makes life difficult. For most outsiders, "sunny" is the adjective that leaps to join itself to "Italy", and the tourist brochures do not lie: Italy in summer has sun to spare, enough to shrivel crops where water is scarce. The winters, though, are cold, even in the south, where high inland plateaux make a mockery of balmy ideas of the "Mediterranean climate". In the north, winter brings fog. Springtime can swell rivers to destructive torrents, and autumns are often parched enough to frighten farmers. "We have

four seasons here," Italians say cynically: "too dry, too cold, too wet and too hot."

Climate and topography are not the only hardships that Italy imposes on its people. Sometimes the very earth beneath their feet assails them. Although in terms of human history Italy can claim immense antiquity, it is a young country geographically: as mountains go, the Alps and Apennines are restive adolescents, and Italy sits squarely on Europe's most active seismic belt. Small earth tremors are almost a daily occurrence, and major earthquakes inflict devastation at depressingly frequent intervals. The Friuli region in the north-east, for example, was severely damaged in 1976, thousands died in the villages around Naples after an upheaval in 1980 and, in 1984, scores of historic little towns in Umbria and the Abruzzi, near Italy's geographic centre, were badly hit.

Italy's lively geology also includes the only active volcanoes in Europe: Stromboli in the Tyrrhenian Sea, Etna in Sicily and Vesuvius near Naples. An eruption of Vesuvius in 79 A.D. destroyed the towns of Pompeii and Herculaneum; nowadays Vesuvius seems almost quiescent, but it has erupted more than once this century.

Pressure of numbers has long added to the strains on the nation. In the mid-19th century, the population was about 20 million; it had risen to about 30 million by 1900. With not enough good

3

agricultural land to go round and virtually no industry to provide employment, Italians had little choice but to emigrate on a massive scale. The early emigrants chose Germany, France and Switzerland, but by the end of the 19th century, Italians were pouring into North and South America at a rate of hundreds of thousands a year. Emigration peaked in 1913, then fell during the inter-war era to almost nothing as New World countries imposed quotas. In the two decades after World War II, the movement from Italy increased

again. Approximately 300,000 Italians emigrated to Australia and more than three million left for other European countries during the same period. Judging the effect of the exodus is difficult, for while many Italians have settled in their new homes for good, a substantial proportion stay there only temporarily. A man may leave Italy for a season, for a few years, even for a working lifetime, only to return to his roots to enjoy his hard-earned cash.

Partly because of the exiles' return, emigration has not succeeded in keep-

ing a lid on the Italian population, which now stands at 57 million. The population density is only average—higher than in France and the United States, lower than in Britain and West Germany—but when set against the scarcity of cultivable or habitable land, it looks high indeed.

Italy's formidable terrain, where it has not actually driven its natives away altogether, has encouraged their segmentation into small, self-contained communities. Mountains do not make for easy communication, and poor

68

communications breed separatism. Local independence was strongest in medieval times, when most of the Italian communes were virtually self-governing. From the 15th century, European power politics divided Italy between rival rulers.

Even today, more than a century after unification, Italians themselves frequently claim that there is no such thing as an Italian: only Lombards and Tuscans, Romans and Apulians, Venetians and Sicilians. They exaggerate. An excellent road network now provides a physical linkage unthinkable even 50 years ago, and television has gone a long way towards standardizing language, attitudes, consumer tastes and dress. Less subtly, the massive internal migrations of the post-war years literally stirred up the population, juxtaposing families with very different traditions and forcing them to find a *modus vivendi*.

But regional loyalties are still very strong, a fact that was recognized in the 1947 republican constitution, which named 19 regions (since increased to 20 by the splitting of Abruzzi-Molise into its two constituent parts) to which certain government functions were to be devolved. Out of the 19 regions, Val d'Aosta, Trentino-Alto Adige, Friuli-Venezia Giulia, Sardinia and Sicily were granted "special" status and by the 1960s had a fair degree of autonomy. In these three frontier zones and two islands, suspicion of central government was especially strong and threats to secede had made a radical move imperative. The remaining regions, however, had to wait until 1970 before they were allowed to elect assemblies empowered to legislate on planning and other regional matters.

Devolved government has under-scored local pride, but even without it regional attachments would have remained very strong. Regional identity exists first and foremost in people's minds; and it finds expression in the infinite gradation of dialect, custom and even cooking that Italy displays.

The differences between dialects were once a real barrier to communication, and they remain striking. The language now known as Italian is essentially the dialect of Tuscany (although the Tuscan accent is not the same as standard Italian). Tuscan is only one of many descendants of the old Latin tongue of the peninsula, but it was the one used by the poet Dante in his 14th-century masterpiece, the *Divina Commedia*. Subsequent Italian writers were deeply influenced by Dante's example, and Tuscan slowly became the language of the intelligentsia. It made virtually no headway as a language for ordinary people, however. At the time of Italian unification, it was spoken as a mother-tongue by less than 3 per cent of the population. Speakers of different dialects could barely comprehend each other. Thus the word *bianco*—white in standard Italian—becomes *biank* in parts of Piedmont, *giancu* in Liguria, *iango* in Campania, *aspro* in southern Calabria and *iancu* in eastern Sicily.

Italian became the language of the new, unified state, and thus the language of compulsory schooling—and of social advancement. Dialects were actively discouraged and regional writers, like everyone else, had to make the best of it. Ignazio Silone, the great novelist of the Abruzzi, summed up the difficulties and resentments of many when he wrote, in 1930, that "the Italian language is for us a foreign language, a dead language, a language whose vocabulary and grammar have no connection with our way of acting, our way of thinking, our way of expressing ourselves." He and others had learnt to use it, of course, but "in the same way that we put on shoes and collar and tie for a visit to the city. Anyone can see our awkwardness."

Even today, Italian is far from being a universal tongue. According to a survey carried out in 1982, only 29 per cent of the population use it at home. The rest of them speak either their traditional dialect or a mixture of that and the newly learnt language.

Social customs, too, vary. Southerners enjoy a long, post-lunchtime nap, for instance, while many northerners work through the afternoon. As far up the boot as Tuscany, the streets are alive on warm nights with families taking the air after dinner; but further north, social life takes place indoors after dark. Italians are conservative about such habits, and "mixed" marriages between spouses of different regions often require a long period of delicate adjustment to new ways.

Adaptation comes hardest, perhaps, in the field of cookery, for food inspires the fiercest regional loyalties. Italian cooking is deservedly world-famous, but if you want to find an Italian restaurant you must seek it out in Britain or in Germany, France or the United States, not in Italy, where local tastes and preferences are strong enough to overwhelm anything that might call itself a national cuisine.

True, pasta in one form or another appears on almost every table; but it arrives in a fantastic profusion of shapes, many of which are firmly associated with a particular region and dismissed as foreign nonsense by the others. And if the pasta is boiled for long enough to satisfy a Milanese, say,

3

then anyone south of Rome will reject it as useless mush.

The risotto beloved of the *milanesi* is virtually unknown in the south; the maize porridge called polenta, much favoured in the north-east, is eyed elsewhere with suspicious distaste; the pungent sauces beloved in the south are considered barbaric in Florence; and so on *ad infinitum*. The proper way to cook things is the way that grandma cooked them; and grandma thought the same.

All this diversity is an endless source of delight to the traveller; it makes a tour of Italy like a journey through a patchwork of little countries, each proudly distinct from its neighbours. Every one of the 20 regions has its own character; they do, however, fall into three broad geographical groupings: the north, the centre and the south.

The north—"European" as opposed to "peninsular" Italy—covers roughly the area between the Alps and the Apennines; it has a history of enterprise and reasonably well-organized government. Its natives see themselves, with some justice, as more purposeful, more go-ahead than other Italians. They are certainly richer. In appearance, they are mostly as dark-haired as the rest of the country's inhabitants, but they tend to be taller than the national average, and blue eyes and even blond hair are not startling rarities.

The centre, encompassing five regions and running more or less from the northern edge of the Apennines to the vicinity of Rome, is not enormously different; the distinction is more one of geographical convenience than a cultural divide. Much of the region spent centuries under the benevolent neglect of papal rule, and its economic advancement suffered correspondingly; but the area was also the birthplace of

the Renaissance, and its inhabitants still like to think of themselves as intellectually superior to all others.

The south is another matter: not so much a geographical description as the statement of a problem that has lurked in the background of Italian politics ever since unification. Historically, the south was the part of Italy which once owed allegiance to the kings of Naples. Economically, it includes the most backward and depressed parts of Italy. Politically it has come to imply—in the eyes of northerners at least—a deep-seated distrust of authority combined with an incorrigible habit of corruption that defies all attempts at assistance. The south, in short, is different. Even its people—smaller and darker than elsewhere, sometimes almost Arab in appearance—seem a different race. Italy stretches more than 1,000 kilometres from top to toe, and the cultural span is many times as long.

A logical place to begin a tour of the country is Piedmont; for, despite its peripheral position in Italy's north-

western corner, it rightly claims to be the political kernel from which the modern nation grew. Italian unification was brought about in the 1850s and 1860s under Piedmont's royal house; for a brief period Turin was the capital of the new state. In the 20th century, the Fiat factories have made Turin a capital of a different sort, the home of Italy's car industry.

Turin stands a little north of the area that produces what are arguably Italy's best wines. The hills around the town of Alba are the heartland of the Nebbiolo, reckoned by wine-lovers to be Italy's noblest grape variety. The name is a reminder of the north's notorious winter fogs—*nebbie*—but there is nothing foggy about the region's powerful and long-matured wines of Barolo and Barbaresco. Many of the vineyards use production methods that have scarcely changed in centuries, at least for their most "serious"—and their most expensive—wines; others have welcomed modern, more scientific techniques largely pioneered in California. Outsiders are unlikely to be able to contribute to the simmering controversy between traditionalists and modernists, since the best Barolos, no matter how they are made, rarely leave Piedmont.

Perhaps it is a pity when they do, for they taste best when accompanying good Piedmontese food: vegetables in a pungent sauce called *bagna cauda*, fine hams and salami, game and, most celebrated of all, the fragrant white truffles from the same hills of Alba that yield the finest Barolo. The Piedmontese are known, with some justice, as "the Prussians of Italy": stern, hard-working and disciplined to a fault. But they are not too stern to enjoy a good table.

Piedmont is not all high; indeed, its name means "at the foot of the mountain". In the Po valley, just west of Turin, graceful lines of poplars separate flourishing wheatfields and orchards, as well as the paddy fields—startlingly un-European in appearance—that furnish two thirds of Italy's rice supply.

The Po valley extends east into the next region—Lombardy, named after the Germanic tribes who colonized it in the Dark Ages. On the northern edge of the plain, Lake Garda, Maggiore and Como provide Europe with some of its most glorious scenery. Gentle hills with lush vegetation flank parts of the lakes, wild cliffs characterize other zones; the soaring Alps are a stunning backdrop.

With almost nine million people, Lombardy is Italy's most populous region and it is also the most productive, accounting for a full third of Italian exports. Its agriculture is similar to Piedmont's, and the Lombards have long made ingenious use of the mighty Po. Since medieval times, a complex system of communally maintained canals has distributed irrigation water and provided protection against the river's regular floods. Leonardo da Vinci made plans for the system's improvement during his spell in the employment of the French ruler of Milan in the early 16th century.

The city of Milan, the capital of Lombardy, houses other products of Leonardo's protean genius, notably his recently restored painting of *The Last Supper* in the convent of Santa Maria delle Grazie. But Milan is better known for engineering, banking and industrial design than for fine art. The city is a brusque and businesslike place, where dazzling new high-rise office blocks jostle for space in elegant 19th-century boulevards and cramped medieval lanes. Along with the stylishness that has made the city a capital of the design world, it exudes a hard-headed self-confidence that has been a Lombard hallmark for centuries.

Italy's second largest city is unchallenged as the "work capital" of the country—at least within earshot of the Milanese, who have little time for the chaotic bureaucracy of Rome.

3

Businessmen point with pride at the number of international companies that have chosen Milan rather than Rome for their headquarters. Anti-Roman feeling is not confined to the managerial classes. In 1984, for example, the English football team Liverpool beat Rome in a European Cup Final: most Italians took the defeat as a minor national calamity, but delighted Milanese graffiti artists blazoned "Thanks, Liverpool" on empty walls.

While Milan strives for success and recognition, Venice, the capital of the Veneto region, is content to bask in former glories. Once the headquarters of a maritime empire, the trade centre where the west met the orient, Venice began to lose its pre-eminence in the 16th century when other nations successfully competed for a share in the trade with the east. Since then, the city has been little more than a glorious museum. Scarcely a modern building jars the eye amid the wonderful jumble of medieval, Renaissance and baroque architecture, and not a car is to be seen. Venice is built on an archipelago of islets in the centre of a salt-water lagoon, and the only form of transport other than legs are the boats that plough along the winding canals.

With its countless bridges dappled with reflections from the water, its brilliant churches with their bell-towers leaning this way and that, its asymmetric squares from which mysterious alleys lead off in all directions, Venice is to many the most entrancing of cities. Others are depressed by its crumbling stone and peeling façades, and by the artificiality of Venice's modern existence. House prices and rents are understandably high. Many of Venice's palaces are owned by foreigners and

Sheep graze below an avenue of Tuscan cypresses, which in mythology provided the wood for Cupid's arrows. In the 1970s, a fungus killed a quarter of the trees. Scientists saved the rest, preserving the traditional landscape of the region, whose contours the trees have defined for centuries.

rich Milanese businessmen, while the humble workers in Venice's tourist industry are often obliged to live in the unlovely mainland suburb of Mestre and then commute in along the causeway each day.

In the Veneto region, which forms the bulk of the old Venetian republic on the Italian mainland, almost every small town still boasts a statue of the Lion of Saint Mark, emblem of the Republic's former might. Now that Venice's real power has vanished, the Veneto's biggest inland cities, Verona and Vicenza, have discovered a new economic centre of gravity in the city of Milan.

Vicenza was the birthplace of the colossally influential 16th-century architect Andrea Palladio. His pedimented, porticoed villas, elegant and harmonious in their proportions, remain among the most admired features of the Veneto's flat, misty landscape, where small farmers grow maize for the polenta that was once their staple diet. Their hold on the land is often tenuous: floods are frequent, especially in the Po delta, where land reclamation schemes struggle to maintain an unstable dominance over the encroaching sea.

Liguria, the last of the northern regions, was once Venice's great maritime rival—the republic of Genoa. Unlike Venice, Genoa never lost its sea legs. It is Italy's biggest port and home of most of the shipbuilding industry— as well as of a people reputed, like the Scots, to be canny and tight-fisted.

The region is not large, a narrow crescent curving round the Mediterranean from the French border to Tuscany. The coast constitutes the Italian Riviera, and its year-round gentle climate has encouraged predictable over-

3

development. Inland lie the Ligurian Apennines, the scene of fierce partisan fighting in World War II but now almost deserted. Over the last 30 years its inhabitants have given up subsistence hill-farming for an easier city life.

Between the mountains and the sea, a whole series of steep valleys descends at right angles to the coast. Intensively terraced since Roman times, they now glitter with greenhouses producing vast quantities of the fresh-cut flowers that are Liguria's most lucrative export. The narrow Ligurian valleys also yield some of Italy's most highly rated olive oil. Less traditional, the coastal autostrada that cuts across their rugged topography winds through a breathtaking succession of tunnels and viaducts that make an impressive advertisement for modern Italian engineering.

The Apennines continue southwards into Emilia-Romagna, the most northerly of the central regions, which extends as far as the Po. About half of its area is mountainous, but most of its principal cities as well as some of the best agricultural land in Italy lie in the fertile Emilian plain. Once it was part of the Papal States, administered directly by the Church. Now it has a well-earned reputation for anti-clericalism. It is also known for its radical politics, which are partly a reaction against the region's landlords, whose large and technically advanced farms for decades employed landless labourers at subsistence wages.

Today, much of Emilia-Romagna exudes prosperity, and Bologna, its capital, is aptly nicknamed La Grassa—"The Fat". Bologna is generally agreed to be the gastronomic capital of Italy. Its specialities are not particularly sophisticated, simply very good: innumerable different kinds of fresh pasta, sometimes flavoured with spinach and often stuffed with meat and vegetables or ricotta cheese, almost invariably served with lashings of excellent cream; mighty plates of boiled meats; and of course the world-famous ham and cheese from nearby Parma.

Beyond Emilia-Romagna, the spine of the Apennines curves towards the Adriatic side of the peninsula. Tuscany lies to the westward, between the ridgeline of the mountains and the Mediterranean Sea. The region is mostly hill country, with a fair share of mountains, and the rolling, richly wooded landscape gives an impression of being gentler than it truly is.

It is first-class wine country, the home of Chianti. Italy's best-known wine is made to a high standard of quality, not least because the average Tuscan producer has become an enthusiastic convert to the new, scientific oenology. Dingy cellars equipped with mouldering 19th-century equipment have become rare, taken over by stainless steel with judiciously applied modern biochemistry. Rivers of Chianti inundate the world, but Tuscany's less abundant wines—which include Vino Nobile di Montepulciano and the highly regarded Brunello di Montalcino—are little known abroad and in fact they rarely travel further from their birthplace than Florence.

Florence, Tuscany's capital, was the main crucible of Renaissance painting; it remains a great cultural centre and an irresistible magnet for lovers of fine art. Although it has acquired an expanding suburbia with a ring of light industries, the old city centre is much as it was in the 15th century, when its ruling Medici family was at the height of its power. Florence's people, too, have changed very little: it can be an uncanny experience to walk from the city's great Uffizi Gallery and then see on the streets outside the same kind of faces that Botticelli or da Vinci painted 500 years before.

Tuscans are something of a race apart. At once imaginative and dour, hardworking and mischievous, they have a reputation for tough bargaining and a certain perverse cunning. According to the Tuscan writer Curzio Malaparte, "... when others weep, we laugh, and when others laugh, we stand and watch them laughing, without batting an eyelid, in silence: until the smile freezes on their lips."

South of Tuscany is the region of Umbria—Italy's green heart, as the area's own publicity justifiably calls it, and the only region that includes neither a sea-coast nor an international frontier. Umbria is predominantly agricultural, and its farming practices are relatively traditional; the mountainous terrain allows only limited scope for the mechanization now typical in the Po valley.

Umbria's greatest asset is the appeal to visitors of its beautiful landscape and the exquisite old towns that cap every likely hill. Perugia, the region's capital, is an almost perfect medieval hill town, naturally compact and preserved as much by civic pride as by Umbria's rigorous planning laws. Orvieto, Gubbio and Spoleto are equally lovely; and Assisi has been a major tourist attraction ever since its beloved Saint Francis died in the 13th century. The town has survived 700 years of pilgrims and sightseers with an aplomb that few modern resorts can match.

The Adriatic coast of northern Italy is itself an unfortunate example of unrestricted tourist development: concrete, concrete and more concrete, in an almost unbroken line from Rimini and Catholica in Emilia-Romagna through Ancona, the regional capital of the Marches, to the mouth of the River Tronto at the Marches' southernmost extremity. The Marches earned its name historically as the border province dividing the corrupt and torpid Papal States to the north from the corrupt and torpid Kingdom of the Two Sicilies to the south; today, the region shares with the south a serious problem of rural depopulation.

But the mountainous interior is not all abandoned farms. Notoriously bad roads—modernized now, but still long and twisting—have protected fine old towns such as Urbino and Loreto from the worst ravages of tourism. The deep valleys and rugged mountain slopes that so impede communication at least give the Marches some of the most impressive scenery in Italy, with specta-

A large herd of oxen fording a stream *(above)* and their dashing *buttero*, or cowboy *(above, left)*, reflect the economy of the Maremma, north of Rome on the west coast. A vast reclamation project drained its malarial marshes, leaving fertile farmland that supports sturdy local breeds of horses and cattle.

3

The medieval silhouette of Orvieto crowns steep cliffs above an Umbrian valley. A 16th-century well in the heart of the mountain assured a water supply in times of siege. The well is in disuse but tourists can descend the shaft by one of the twin spiral staircases built for the water-laden donkeys.

cular waterfalls and grottoes. It is the kind of landscape that encourages independence, and on the edge of the Marches is a quaint historical anomaly that still defies the process of Italian unification: the miniature independent republic of San Marino, whose 61 square kilometres support a population of around 20,000, a government and even a tiny standing army.

Real government, of course, is the business of Rome, across the Apennines in the region of Latium—though Rome, too, has its comic-opera aspects. As the English newspaperman Peter Nichols wrote perceptively: "To the south, it personifies the heartless concentration of power which the southerner regards as constantly working against his due interests; to the north it is an intolerable burden which is holding back the development of enterprise and modern society, like some elderly, overdressed, self-centred old mistress who refuses to give way to the new young wife." But provincials have complained about Rome for rather more than 2,000 years, and Rome has usually managed to fascinate and seduce its critics: the Eternal City did not get its name for nothing.

After the glorious days of the Roman Republic and Empire, the invasions of Vandals, Goths and other barbarians temporarily put Rome out of business. But before long it found a new lease of life as headquarters of the Catholic Church. It did not become part of modern, united Italy until 1870, nine years after the rest of the country had come together, but it was then the inevitable choice as capital. The city enjoyed a tremendous upsurge in public building in the late 19th century as each ministry vied with every other to provide itself with headquarters accommodation for its essential bureaucrats—a process that has continued until the present day.

But Rome remains above all a city of the 17th century—the heyday of papal splendour, when baroque sculptors adorned every skyline with gesticulating saints. As the English travel writer H. V. Morton remarked, "The Rome that first prints itself upon the eye and the mind is not classical Rome, buried beneath the streets and covered with its shroud of Time, or medieval Rome, which now consists mainly of a stray and lovely campanile, or 19th-century gigantism, or modern Rome, a mostly hideous mass of concrete, but this gay, declamatory Rome of the Popes, with its peachy, golden palaces, its once quiet piazze, its glorious fountains and its look of just having happened on some happy and fortunate day."

Officially, the Church no longer rules the city—only the tiny statelet of the Vatican, where about a thousand permanent residents and 3,500 outside workers administer its worldwide congregation and attend to the floods of daily visitors who assail it every day. Some come as pilgrims, others as tourists eager to gaze at the famous frescoes by Michelangelo and Raphael.

With its two bureaucracies and its massive tourist industry, Rome appears to have an insatiable appetite for people. From a peak population of around a million in classical times, it shrank to well under 30,000 in the Middle Ages. But now it is Italy's largest city, with close to three million residents. It lures them from Latium and elsewhere, and rapidly turns them into authentic *romani*, wry and street-wise.

To the east and south of Rome, Italy's real problems begin. This is the zone of

3

hardship, from which millions have fled in search of a better life either in the cities or abroad.

As the crow flies, the mountainous Abruzzi region, on a latitude with Latium, is not far from Rome; but until an autostrada link was built in 1970, the journey on the ground was a long one, across the highest point in the whole Apennine chain. The isolation of the Abruzzi people no doubt helped them acquire their unmerited reputation as the comic dimwits of Italy.

Traditionally, sheep-rearing provided a scanty living here as in neighbouring Molise. Now, however, a winter sports industry is being built up, and the Abruzzi National Park attracts patient nature watchers hoping to catch a glimpse of its rarest and its most renowned denizens, the brown bear and the Apennine wolf.

Campania, south of Latium, provides a startling contrast to the windswept mountains of Abruzzi and Molise. In the summer, driving towards Naples from Rome is like driving into a furnace. Tree-clad hills give way to scrub slopes and bare earth, cactus begins to proliferate by the roadside, and the soil itself changes from a familiar European brown to a sullen, tropical red.

But where there is water, the soil is fertile enough. The Campanian plain is a gigantic kitchen garden, producing peas and beans, peppers, tomatoes, aubergines and assorted fruits in its volcanically enriched earth. It is also the home of the principal consumers of this wealth of produce: the residents of the astonishing city of Naples.

Naples is teeming. Most of its population of well over a million can aspire at best to a cramped little flat, and many of them are condemned to the worst slum housing in Europe. In com-

Roman traffic crawls along the Via della Conciliazione in front of St. Peter's Basilica. To create such broad vistas and the triumphal parade routes that are a feature of modern Rome, Mussolini demolished much of the medieval city in the 1930s.

pensation, they live the best part of their lives on the streets. The city is full of cars, from purring Mercedes to battered old Fiat 500s, co-existing with the people in a peculiarly Neapolitan way. "You have to stop at the green lights here," warned a driver. "In Naples, you can be sure that someone will be going through the red." It hardly needs saying that Naples is also full of noise.

Despite the factories and refineries that disfigure the once-glorious Bay of Naples, there is by no means enough work for the city's inhabitants. Many can only hope to live by the celebrated Neapolitan art of "getting by": an odd hour's labouring here, an afternoon as an unlicensed taxi-driver there, a little dealing somewhere else and perhaps, if no one is looking, a lucky find—a carelessly chained bicycle, say, or a tourist's handbag. And there is contraband on a gigantic scale. At night, powerful launches bring smuggled cigarettes and other goods into the city's harbour. In the daytime, people sell them openly in the streets, ignored by the police. Contraband makes fortunes for a few gang leaders and a handful of corrupt

politicians. More to the point, it provides a modest living for thousands of Neapolitans who would otherwise be destitute, desperate and dangerous. It is no wonder that the authorities choose to turn a blind eye: Naples lives on the edge of a volcano in more than one sense, and one day it could well be the city itself that erupts, not smoky old Vesuvius above it.

South of Naples is the beautiful Sorrento peninsula with its steep cliffs rising from an azure sea, its olive and citrus groves. Tourism has long sustained the inhabitants both here and on the island of Capri, which is only 5 kilometres from the southern tip of the Sorrento peninsula.

The mountainous island is blessed with luxuriant vegetation and a limpid atmosphere. For a place of extraordinary tranquillity and beauty, Capri hides an unexpectedly sinister past. The Roman Emperor Tiberius was seduced by the charms of the place in 27 A.D.; up until then, he had reigned wisely and beneficently, but the story of his 10-year sojourn on the island is not an edifying one. According to contemporary writers, he amused himself on Capri with every sort of cruel and obscene entertainment. He built a dozen great villas on the perimeter of Capri, and incorporated into them dungeons, torture chambers and places of execution; in one villa which has been excavated, some of these macabre spots can be visited today.

Calabria, the narrow toe of the Italian boot, has Italy's most spectacular coastline, but voracious, unplanned development is blighting many parts of it that are not protected by sheer cliffs. In addition to hotels and holiday villas, there are dozens of ugly skeletons of half-completed houses. These are the

work of Calabrian emigrants who return for a week or two each year, if
money permits, and build a little more
of the home they hope to retire to.

Calabria was once a Greek colony,
and the local dialect, guttural and im-
penetrable to outsiders, still owes as
much to Greek as to Latin. Even odder
is the fact that, buried deep in the
mountains, there are villages of Albanian speakers. These communities date
back to the 15th century, when the
ancestors of the present inhabitants
were refugees from the Turkish conquest of their land. Their successors
have managed to retain their cultural
identity for two reasons: physical isolation, of course, but also the fact that
they are descended from the cream of
the Albanian nation, people who had
fought their conquerors bitterly and
emigrated only when the last battles
had been lost.

Basilicata, the instep of Italy, is the
south at its cruellest. Stark with hills as
bare as slag-heaps, the landscape looks
like spoil from some monstrous excavation, and the grim little towns that are
huddled together on the hilltops seem
no more than the last of the earth's
leavings. Rivers, for most of the year,
are little more than grey beds of gravel,
waiting to serve simply as run-offs for
the ferocious autumn rains which never
come to nourish the land, only to scour
it mercilessly.

The countryside has few farmhouses.
Such people as remain—Basilicata's
population has fallen steadily for 40
years—live cheek by jowl in cramped
towns that are little more than barracks
for agricultural labourers. Each morning before dawn, men and women alike
set off together to walk great distances
to their wretched fields; each evening,

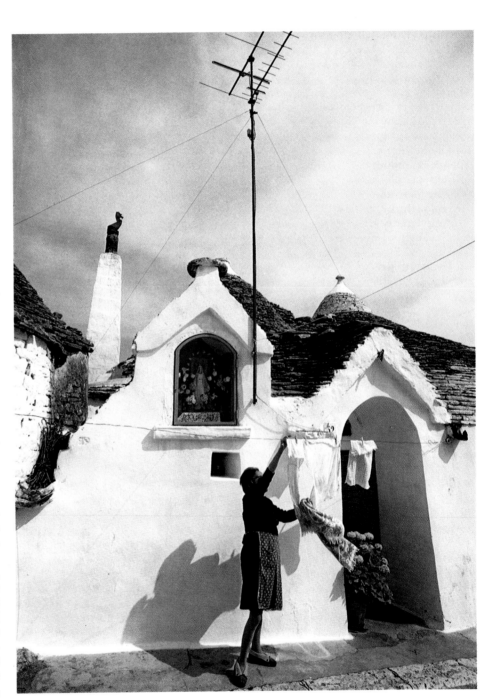

A woman takes down washing outside
her *trullo*, a whitewashed stone dwelling
of ancient design found only in Apulia,
Italy's heel. Perfectly suited to a hot
climate, the building's thick walls keep
its interior cool and the conical roof
channels precious rain to a cistern.

3

after dusk, they return home.

In her book *Women of the Shadows*, the fruit of 20 years' intimate acquaintance with the peasants of Basilicata, the American Ann Cornelisen writes:

To go to the fields is almost a reflex, conditioned by the absolute lack of any other work. You go, even when you might not have to. The donkey needs fodder: you cut it by hand, sometimes just along the verges, and shove it into the sacks that hang from the saddle. While you're about it, you pull up wild greens for a salad—a little sorrel, dandelions, whatever there is. You weed your patch of wheat, you loosen the dirt around the beans, tie up a vine. You look over to see how your neighbor's crops are coming. Not really that you hoped yesterday's hailstorm had beaten them down, but there would be some justice if. . . You collect a few twigs for kindling. And finally at some invisible cue of light not yet changed but about to change, the long walk back to town. Five miles, ten—a long way with nothing to think about except how to get a bit more land, a job—how to feed your children. Your children. Will they live like this? You don't ride the donkey; he needs his strength too. The click of his hooves, the scrape of your boots and you almost fall asleep walking.

Weather permitting, everyone spends their leisure time in the streets—often unpaved and furnished with an open sewer. Men sit gossiping, surveying the outside world, while women turn their backs to it and knit, compelled by custom to dress in black and face the crumbling walls of their houses.

Even in Basilicata, however, the picture is not one of unrelieved wretchedness. In the town of Matera, for instance, most of the population used to live, livestock and all, in the *sassi*—a honeycomb of little caves. Now the *sassi* are almost empty, and a bright new town has sprung into life above and around them. Some of the new prosperity is based on money sent home by emigrants working in the north, but government investment is responsible for launching a few local industries too. Matera's shops are well stocked and always have plenty of customers.

Of the three southernmost regions, only Apulia—the heel of Italy—has managed to achieve anything like real economic success. Its natural advantages are considerable: more than half of its area is flat and, despite a chronic water shortage, much of the land is as fertile as any other region in Italy. Vines, fruit and olive trees as bulky as small oaks have been growing in Apulia for centuries; industry, too, has a relatively long history. Taranto has been a strategic naval base for Italy since the Suez Canal was opened in 1869; with Brindisi and the regional capital of Bari, it forms part of an industrial triangle that is strong in petrochemicals and steel.

The five so-called "special regions" of Italy owe their greater autonomy—and the earlier date of their receiving it—to special problems. The three northern units—Val d'Aosta, Trentino-Alto Adige and Friuli-Venezia Giulia—are all frontier regions with their own history of dissenting minorities; the islands of Sicily and Sardinia came out of the Second World War seething with secessionist resentment because of their years of neglect at the hands of the central administration.

Val d'Aosta is the smallest of all the regions, an enclave in the high Alps around Mont Blanc. French used to be the inhabitants' principal language. The growth of a winter sports industry has largely halted a worrying decline in its population; local autonomy, and a reasonable level of material well-being, have greatly weakened its still-active separatist movement.

Trentino-Alto Adige's situation is more complex. The German-speaking province of Alto Adige (otherwise known as the South Tyrol) was Italy's main reward for victory over Austria in World War I. Many of its inhabitants were less than enthusiastic about the transfer of sovereignty, especially when Mussolini's Fascist government directed a stream of immigrants into the province in order to inflate the Italian-speaking minority. Mussolini also banned German speakers from public office and refused to permit German surnames to be used.

Unsurprisingly, then, the leaders of the post-war Italian Republic had some very unhappy and suspicious people to deal with. In the end, a hybrid region was created that included the Italian-speaking area of Trentino. Alto Adige and Trentino, as well as the region as a whole, were each allowed to control their own administration.

But the creation of a region with an overall Italian majority did nothing to mollify the German speakers in the Alto Adige. In the 1960s, they turned to violence and succeeded in gaining more power for themselves and more protection for their language. Since then, the region has settled down, the old conflicts still simmering but masked by the general prosperity of both its parts.

That other composite region, Friuli-Venezia Giulia, grew out of the need to provide a hinterland for the ailing port of Trieste, which almost became part of Yugoslavia at the end of World War II. Trieste is a beautiful, haunted city; its *raison d'être* vanished with the Austro-

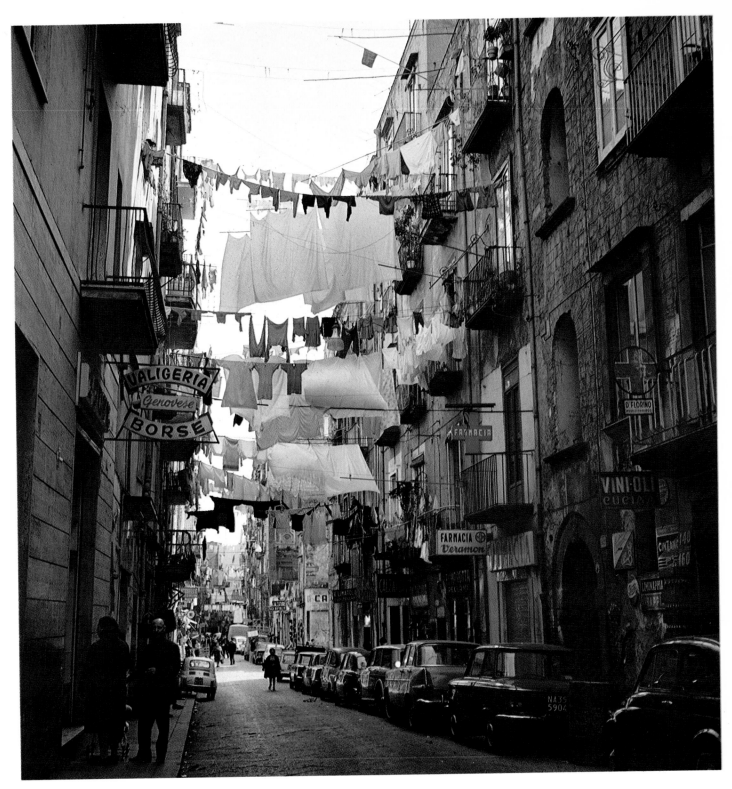

Streamers of laundry garland a narrow
street in Naples, the most densely
populated city in Europe. In recent
years, local authorities have built much
housing on the periphery of the city,
but some 100,000 Neapolitans still live
in one-room dwellings in the centre.

3

Hungarian Empire, for which it was once the major outlet. Italians have, however, always been deeply attached to the place.

The region is a highly artificial creation. Venezia Giulia is all that remains of a much larger province which once included the peninsula of Istria, successfully claimed by Yugoslavia in the post-war settlement; the agricultural territory known as Friuli has traditional links with Venice rather than Trieste. The area's economy was somewhat moribund even before the 1976 earthquake, which devastated several villages and badly damaged the historic city of Udine.

Sicily, at least, is not artificial; indeed no one could possibly have invented this island. It is the largest of all the Italian regions and, with approximately five million people, it is also one of the more populous. It does possess

some advantages: reasonably good land, though often poorly watered, and mineral reserves that are plentiful, at least by Italian standards. But Sicily's regional government has been an unmitigated disaster, afflicted by chronic corruption and *clientelismo*—which is the habit of distributing jobs and contracts as political patronage.

The island—at any rate, its western half and the regional capital of Palermo—is also the home of the Mafia, and the clammy hand of criminal conspiracy is largely responsible for the poor state of local industry and the high level of emigration.

Yet Sicily has made an immense contribution to Italian culture—especially, in modern times at least, to Italian literature. From Luigi Pirandello, the influential playwright who probed the boundary between reality and illusion, to the Nobel prize-

winning poet Salvatore Quasimodo, Sicily's writers have given their homeland a powerful voice.

Many of these writers have found their themes in the island's social distress: in the novel *Mastro-don Gesualdo*, for example, the 19th-century author Giovanni Verga set his obsessively ambitious hero against the bitter realities of the poverty-stricken island. More recently, the shrewd and observant novels of Leonardo Sciascia have managed to penetrate to the very heart of the present-day Mafia.

Sicily is also remarkable for the number of outstanding, honest politicians it has exported—as opposed to the less-than-upright examples who remain at home. Riccardo Lombardi, from Enna in the centre of the island, was a famous partisan during World War II and a key member of the Socialist Party until his death in 1984. Somewhat to the left of his party's centre, Lombardi involved himself fiercely and passionately in every issue, but lacked the ruthless personal ambition that tempted many of his colleagues into corruption. Ugo La Malfa, from Palermo, was for many years the leader of the small Republican Party. He shaped it into an organ that has earned universal respect for its thoughtful policies and high standards.

Italy's other great Mediterranean island, Sardinia, has also sent some of its best political minds to the mainland—most notably Enrico Berlinguer, who until his death in 1984 was the popular leader of the Italian Communist Party. Generally, though, Sardinia has kept itself to itself, in an isolation that has been anything but splendid.

The island is a poor place even now, mountainous and lacking in good inland roads. Many of its inhabitants are

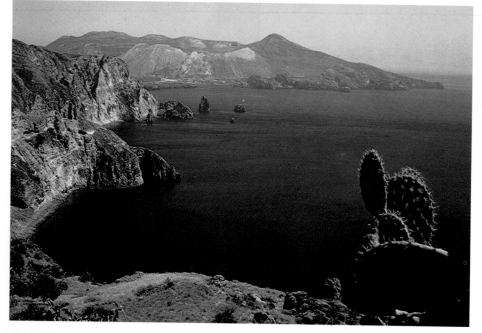

The brilliant blue waters of the Tyrrhenian Sea lap the sharply hewn coast of Lipari Island in the Aeolian archipelago north of Sicily. The island's volcanic rock has provided profitable exports over the centuries: glass-like obsidian in ancient times and abrasive pumice stone today.

Volcanic Mount Etna, whose name comes from the Greek for "I burn", smoulders above Taormina, a Sicilian resort town. Europe's largest volcano, it erupts on average more than once a decade. In 1928, its lava flow buried the nearby town of Mascali.

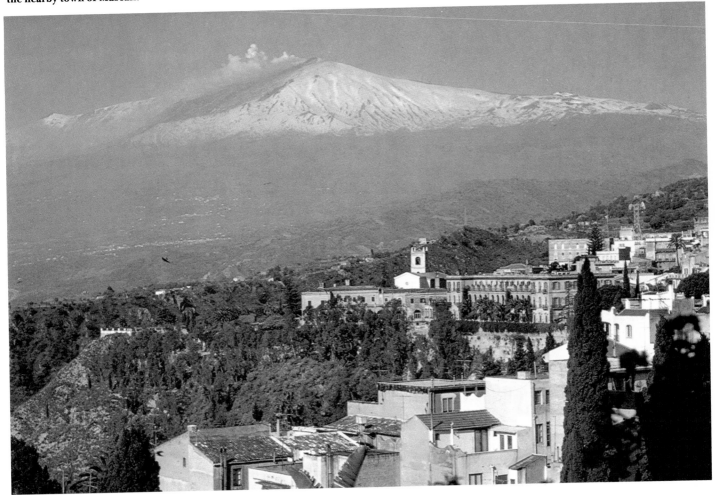

still shepherds, following their flocks in semi-nomadic fashion across the high pastures of the interior. Sardinia's sharp and well-matured sheep's-milk cheeses are renowned throughout Italy; and so are its bandits, with their tradition of robbery and kidnapping. Unlike Sicily's *mafiosi*, however, who batten sleekly on the wealth of an organized society, Sardinian bandits are the outward manifestation of a hard life, close to the margins of survival, embodying cruel but ancient traditions of honour and vendetta.

Still, a killer is a killer, whether he is dressed in a smart grey suit or a rough sheepskin jerkin. No one is sorry that banditry on Sardinia is gradually dying out—least of all the growing number of people there who now depend on the tourist industry for their living. For the moment, kidnapping remains a lucrative business on the island, but in time economic development may make banditry an obsolete occupation.

It is unlikely to make Sardinians any less Sardinian, dour and remote, but nobody is asking them to change their essential ways. Italians have realized that uniformity is unattainable, at least in the short term; regional feeling runs too deep. Rather than striving towards standardization, they have made a virtue of their diversity. They relish their local cooking, their dialect literature. They are at ease with their differences.

83

RIGOURS OF LIFE IN THE FORSAKEN SOUTH

Poverty and endless toil have always been the lot of peasants throughout southern Italy, but hardship is at its most acute in Basilicata, the instep of the Italian boot. The harsh life of the region has never been more vividly portrayed than in the book *Christ Stopped at Eboli* written over 40 years ago by Carlo Levi. The title is drawn from a local way of describing the god-forsaken remoteness of the land south of Eboli.

Levi, an artist and doctor, was exiled to the south in 1935 for his opposition to Mussolini's invasion of Abyssinia. He lived first in the small town of Grassano, but was later moved to the village of Aliano—Gagliano in his book—where his humanity and medical training brought him into close contact with the peasants, who were plagued by malaria and the diseases of want.

Since Levi's sojourn in Basilicata, new roads and irrigation systems have been built, and state industries have brought some new employment. Prosperity, however, has proved elusive. Were Levi alive, he might still write of "this shadowy land . . . where evil is not moral but is only the pain residing forever in earthly things".

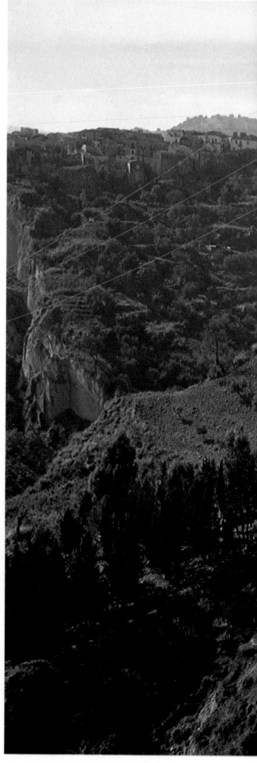

Aliano's priest indulges in a moment of banter with four women who have been picking tomatoes in fields near the village. The priest, faced with high unemployment among Aliano's youth, set up an agricultural co-operative in the late 1970s; it has had some success, despite the area's poor soil.

84

Below the village of Aliano, trees and scrub cling precariously to the unstable clay soil of steep ravines. The villagers must contend not only with erosion but also with earthquakes—one of which destroyed one in three of Aliano's houses in 1980.

Caves at the base of a cliff near Aliano *(above)* serve to store implements and to shelter newborn kids and their mothers. Other goats are penned overnight beneath the rockface *(right)*. In Levi's day, the peasants lived almost entirely off these beasts, which need no pastures, but browse on the area's thorny bushes. Today, they remain a mainstay of the village's economy: their milk is sold to a consortium and then to industry for cheese-making.

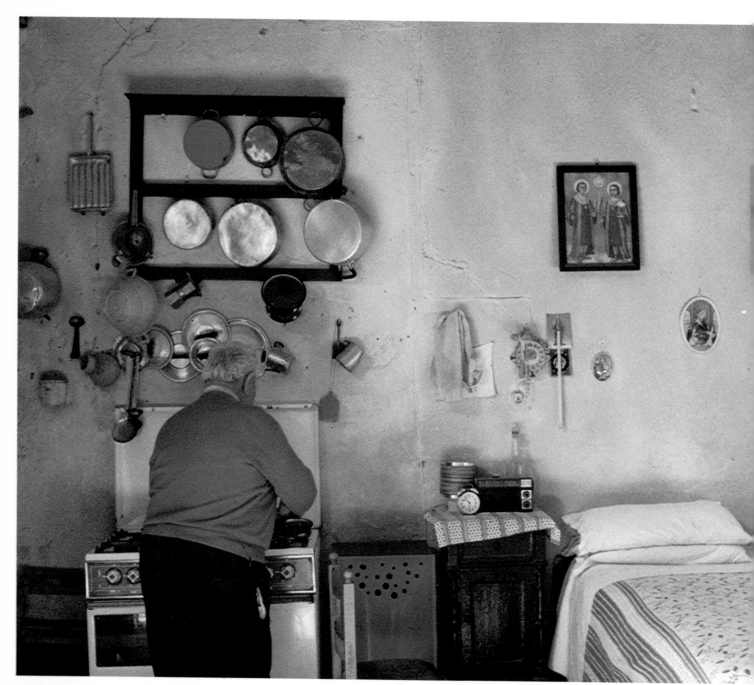

In Grassano, an elderly man prepares a meal in his one-roomed home. Houses have changed little since Levi wrote: "They were all alike... one room almost entirely filled by an enormous bed... in it slept the whole family...". In those days, animals shared the living space; today, goats are kept outside.

Bright modern clothes of a younger generation contrast sharply with the widow's weeds of peasant women in a Grassano street. The older villagers, who grew up with constant hunger and deprivation, are noticeably shorter than the children of post-war years.

A woman waits outside a modernized house in a village near Grassano, while a mule stands under the archway. Most of the villagers farm scattered pieces of land in the hills nearby, where mules and donkeys often work more efficiently than machinery.

An old farm near Matera, the capital of Basilicata, is dwarfed by a chemical complex on its doorstep. This industrial plant is still running—unlike many others zealously set up in the south in the post-war years that fell victim to fluctuations in demand.

In the old part of Matera, stone façades mask cave dwellings cut into the steep hill. Now mostly deserted, the caves used to house whole families in Levi's time, together with their goats and pigs, in overcrowded squalor.

4

AN INSTINCT FOR DRAMA

The Italians have a genius for drama that manifests itself in both their arts and their everyday life. The people who invented opera and infused painting with a new power of expression during the Renaissance know instinctively how to maximize an artistic or emotional effect, how to vitalize a scene with movement and energy. Italian speech, in all its melodiousness, is incomplete without an accompaniment of emphatic gestures and facial expressions—that turn ordinary moments into a kind of theatrical performance.

An important facet of this gift for drama is summed up by the expression *bella figura*. It means style, making the best of yourself, conveying a pleasing impression of yourself to others. *Bella figura* is carefully cultivated and earned by hard work. Many of the Italians are blessed with good looks to begin with, and they take care to enhance their beauty by walking with pride, speaking with fluency and assurance, and, if they can possibly afford to do so, dressing in the latest fashion, even if it means having to skimp on personal comforts. Clothes are a vitally important medium for sending out a personal message to the world. Fashion dictates that everyone who can manage it appears in a new outfit at least twice a year, and that means finding one's own particular niche in the season's prescribed canon of colour and shapes.

This penchant for dramatically costumed entrances and exits plays squarely into the hands of the clothes designers, who have made Italy one of the homes of high fashion ever since the end of World War II. While the panjandrums of Parisian *haute couture* were busy blowing up a fresh storm each year, the Rome of Valentino and Antonelli became the Eternal City of elegance, producing its collections with an aristocratic detachment and a never-failing eye for detail.

Florence is another of Italy's fashion centres—as befits the city whose Renaissance art patrons had built their fortunes on weaving and the cloth trade. But Milan is now undoubtedly Italy's couture capital. Its many famous design houses—Missoni, Armani, Versace and Krizia are just four of the best—specialize in casual elegance. They are as famous for their ravishing fabrics as for the cut of their garments. Sumptuous leather outfits and stylish knitwear are among their fortes.

Deriving so much pleasure from the ever-changing tableau of fashion, Italians also love fancy dress, and have ample opportunity to enjoy it. In Rome, objects of universal admiration are the Pope's Swiss guards, whose uniform is a dazzling assemblage of yellow, red and blue, artfully arranged in individual ribbons of colour. Not to be outdone, the president of the Republic, in the Quirinale Palace, is guarded by a corps of extra-tall cavalrymen, resplendent in steel breastplates, plumed hats and huge sabres. The various units of

As her gondola glides alongside moorings in the Venetian lagoon, a spectral reveller alights to join in the pre-Lent festivities of the annual Carnival. The eerie anonymity of the veil and mask gives her the freedom that thieves, gamblers and lovers have enjoyed for centuries during Carnival.

93

A stylish woman saunters through an appreciative crowd with typically Italian panache. Her confident air helps guarantee her success because, as the Neapolitan film star Sophia Loren once said, "Any woman can convince herself into being more beautiful."

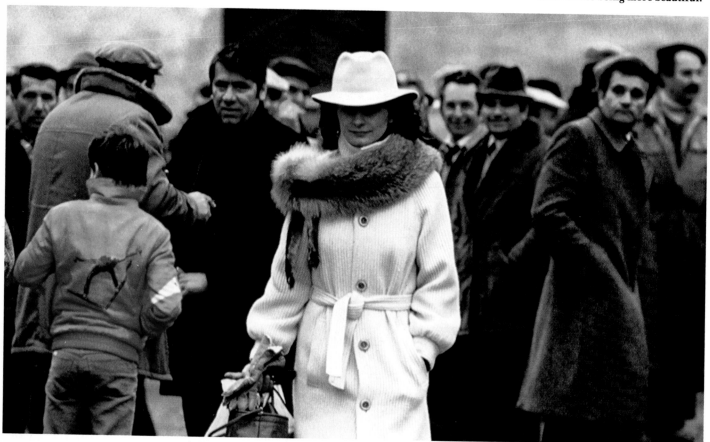

the army, navy and air force pride themselves on wearing a fantastic variety of dress uniforms harking back to earlier epochs of Italian history. The crack regiment of sharpshooters in the army, the bersaglieri, wear great bunches of iridescent feathers in their mountaineers' hats, while the armed police or *carabinieri*, when on ceremonial duty, become the cynosure of all eyes in their Napoleonic-era finery, complete with crossed bandoliers and broad black hats.

In one way or another, nearly everybody has the opportunity to appear several times a year as an actor or extra in some local piece of street theatre, be it a festival or a historical commemoration. During the first week in January, many of the communities sponsor "living pageants" of the arrival of the Magi for the feast of the Three Kings. At Easter time there are countless Good Friday celebrations throughout Italy: Taranto, for example, is famous for its parade of hooded penitents and flagellants, who take 14 hours to make the rounds of the city. On Ascension Day at Cocullo, in the region of Abruzzi, local tradition calls for a "serpent proces-sion" in which pilgrims and singers carry live snakes in their hands, and the image of the patron saint, San Domenico, is ringed with vipers.

In July the Venetians celebrate the end of the plague of 1576 by building a bridge of boats across the wide canal of the Giudecca to the Church of the Redemption, with nocturnal fireworks and concerts in the courtyard of the Doge's Palace. In September the town of Arezzo stages mock jousting against dummy Saracens.

Three times a year, in May, September and December, the whole of

Naples turns out to bear witness to the Miracle of San Gennaro, the local patron saint whose dried blood, kept in two glass phials in a chapel of the cathedral, is supposed to liquefy for the occasion. If the miracle does not occur, disaster for Naples is said to be imminent—but rarely do the officiating clergy fail to announce that the transformation has indeed come about.

The most celebrated and spectacular of all these festivities is the annual Carnival, which is held during the period that precedes Lent. In recent years Venice has recaptured its position as one of the world's favourite venues for such merrymaking.

During the 18th century, the city boasted the longest and the most licentious of all the European carnivals, but in the more sober age that followed, the tradition was allowed to fall into disuse. It was resurrected in the early 1980s, ostensibly for the benefit of the tourist industry, but more likely because the Venetians themselves felt the need for another opportunity to dress up and let off steam.

For 10 frenzied days, inhibitions are thrown to the winds as masked, costumed revellers crowd into the narrow alleys and windy piazzas of the city that was once the merchant capital of the eastern Mediterranean. At the height of the celebrations, as many as 80,000 people fill the great square in front of St. Mark's Basilica.

In earlier centuries, however, Rome was the real headquarters of the Carnival, and many of the popes actively encouraged the custom. The Roman festivities involved pageants, races, banquets and theatrical performances as well as the traditional street jollifications, with costumed crowds singing coarse ditties while pelting each other with sweetmeats. One of the highlights was a race of riderless Berber horses along the broad street known to this day as the Corso, or racecourse. The horses were led in amid shouts and yells from the crowd; strips of tinsel were fastened to their backs and lead balls spiked with needles dangled from their sides, spurring them to a frenzy. A furious struggle ensued as the grooms tried to restrain the animals until, at a signal, the starter's rope fell to the ground and the horses charged pell-mell down the street. At the finishing line, another set of grooms had the unenviable job of catching and controlling the maddened beasts.

When the German poet Goethe visited Rome in the 1780s, this astonishing spectacle struck him as the perfect symbol of the unbridled sensuality that reigned among the people at Carnival time. Because he was well read in the history of ancient Rome, he realized that the celebration he had just witnessed was simply a latter-day version of the equally licentious Saturnalia, the week-long festival in honour of the pagan god Saturn, when sexuality ran rampant, all distinctions of rank were set aside and everyone enjoyed a topsy-turvy freedom of expression. The Carnival was therefore one powerful instance, not only of the Italians' inborn sense of theatre, but of their instinct for cultural continuity. Perhaps no other people in Europe maintain a more intimate relationship with their distant past.

While carnivals and pageants bring history to life in Italy's streets, time-honoured dramatic forms flourish on its stages. The works of a few playwrights from the past, such as the 18th-century Venetian writer of comedies, Carlo Goldoni, are still performed today. However, the most pervasive legacies from other eras are musical drama—that is, opera—and traditional theatrical modes that depend on actors improvising around classical plots and stock characters.

One version of extempore drama that survives today is the puppet theatre of Sicily—a thriving tradition that has hardly changed for centuries. The brilliantly painted marionettes stand about 75 centimetres tall and weigh up to 20 kilograms, so that they have to be manoeuvred by strong handlers working iron rods as well as strings. The voices are supplied by puppeteers whose families have usually been involved in the puppet theatre for a hundred years or more.

Among their stock characters are puppet knights that are fully armed and capable of drawing their swords from their scabbards to fight the classic battles of chivalry—against serpents, villains, giants and Saracens on behalf of truth, justice and the honour of fair damsels. A favourite vehicle for such action is Ariosto's *Orlando Furioso*, the great 16th-century adaptation of the legend of the knight Roland doing battle with the enemies of Christendom. An even more kinetic drama enacts the wholesale slaughter of French invaders by native Sicilians in 1282; the so-called Sicilian Vespers is one instance of the struggle against outside oppressors that has always been the central theme of the island's history. Strong men have been known to weep real tears because these performances evoke the passions and fantasies of their thirst for justice and revenge.

The puppets' fast physical and verbal footwork is paralleled in another Italian tradition, that of the *commedia*

Outraged, reassuring, triumphant, imploring—Italians young and old express their emotions through gesture. The language of the hands and face is rich and subtle: among the Neapolitans alone, one lifelong observer counted 13 different movements meaning "No!"

dell'arte, which first made its appearance in about 1530. It was a frothy, exciting kind of theatre; unlike the amateur theatricals popular at the Renaissance courts, it required arts and skills that only professionals could muster: not only acting, singing, dancing and fencing, but also such sidelines as juggling, conjuring and acrobatics. Handstands and cartwheels were an integral part of the action.

The plays were improvised around stock situations—a rich man is bested by his cunning valet, who also makes off with the beautiful girl, for example—but the plots were of secondary importance. What mattered was the speed, surprise and comedy generated by the cast—a minimum of eight recurring characters who between them represented a spectrum of human, all-too human, foibles and follies.

There was Zanni the comic servant, clever, greedy and shameless, and always in revolt against oppression and injustice. One variation on the Zanni character was the wily Arlecchino (Harlequin), portrayed as a valet who carried a rabbit's tail as the emblem of his courage and wore a patched-up coat of many colours; a second was the crooked-nose, ill-mannered Pulcinella, later to beget the English Mr. Punch. Other characters included Pantalone—a pompous, opinionated Venetian merchant—and a military captain known variously as Spavento, Giangurgolo, Il Vappo or Rogantino—a cowardly swaggerer forever boasting of his past exploits. On the distaff side there was Columbina, a pert and lovely creature in ravishing décolletage, who provided these outrageous farces with an element of love-interest.

Theatre historians searching for the origins of these characters found that their progenitors were much older than the Renaissance. In the Italian arts all roads lead back to ancient Rome: in this case, the starting point was the Atellan farce, a genre of sketches about country bumpkins and city slickers, including Maccus the fool, Manducus the glutton, Pappus the ridiculous old man and Dossennus the wily sharper. Originating around the town of Atella in Campania, the form was taken up by the Romans in the third century B.C. and enjoyed for more than two centuries. The Romans added their own polish and even wrote down some of the scripts, but they always kept a rustic coarseness of language and incident.

The Atellan farce was eventually submerged by other kinds of comedy, but when it resurfaced centuries later as the *commedia dell'arte* it made a profound impact on European theatre. In the 1570s, as an insurance against homesickness, the great Italian heiress Catherine de' Medici, who had gone to Paris to marry the heir to the French throne, afterwards Henry II, invited a *commedia* troupe to come to France to perform for her. Decades later, the

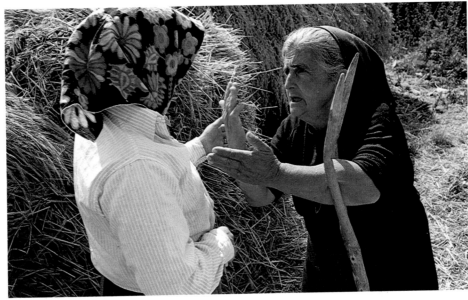

French playwright Molière was enchanted by the actors, and he used some of their tricks and stock situations in his comedies. Before long, their vogue spread to the rest of 16th-century Europe, notably Germany, Russia and England, all of which were visited by companies of Italian players. Today, there is no permanent *commedia* company in Italy, but the form lives on elsewhere: the world's oldest surviving *commedia*-style troupe performs in the Copenhagen pleasure park known as the Tivoli Gardens.

The *commedia* characters have contributed hugely to other forms of theatre, and none more generously than the madcap Zanni. Both circus acts and slapstick comedy depend on borrowings from his repertoire. The world-famous comics of film and television in the 20th-century—Charlie Chaplin, the Marx Brothers, the Keystone Cops and Monty Python—can trace their genealogy directly back to him. And at home in Italy, Zanni and his companions have enriched that other great indigenous dramatic form, the opera.

Opera was invented in Florence in about 1600, when several enterprising musician-poets began experimenting with dramas set to music. Until then the Italian genius for singing had expressed itself in other forms of vocal music, ranging from masses to madrigals. Soon Claudio Monteverdi, composer to the court of Mantua and later master of music in Venice, took up the new musical drama. In his operas, based on classical stories such as the legend of Orpheus, the music responds to every twist in the plot, every change of mood. When Monteverdi had demonstrated what could be done with "the passionate style", as he called it, the rest of Italy quickly adopted opera as a favourite national pastime.

Before long there were opera houses in even the smallest towns and cities, filled with audiences who were avid for new works, and as fervent about opera as modern teenagers are about rock groups. No other country could boast such enthusiastic and knowledgeable music-lovers. They provided the economic base for the steady stream of new operas that began to flow from the pens of dozens of Italian composers. The French novelist Stendhal came to Italy in 1800 with Napoleon's armies and marvelled at the excitement that opera could generate there.

Whenever an opera was to be performed, even in a small town, Stendhal observed, it seemed that the entire population was talking about it for days in advance. On the night of the production, the theatre would be filled to bursting point. Crowds would come pouring into town from miles around; all rooms at the inns would be taken, and some people would be obliged to bivouac in their own carriages while waiting for the doors of the theatre to

4

A cluster of *carabinieri*, members of one of Italy's three police forces, display their blue and scarlet finery. The military dash of this full-dress uniform has changed little since the first officers wore it in 1814. On regular duty, the division dresses in subdued, but well-cut, blue.

open. "The passions, the anxieties, the whole life of a thriving community is focused on its theatre."

Stendhal compared the passionately committed audience at an Italian premiere to the blasé opera-goers of Paris, who were accustomed to sitting on their hands and looking sideways at their neighbours to see what others were thinking about the music. In Italy, "When the overture begins you could hear a pin drop. When it ends the storm bursts: the work is either extolled to the skies or sent to perdition with whistles and catcalls."

The darling of the audiences in Stendhal's time was Gioacchino Rossini, who wrote more than 40 operas—the best of which are comedies—in just over two decades. He was only 24 when he brought forth his masterpiece, *The Barber of Seville*, in 1816. By his own account, it took him 16 days to set down the score. The music seems to move with the same speed and fluency with which it was written; it bubbles and seethes with high-jinks and satire. Much of the action is descended in a direct line from the *commedia dell'arte*. Figaro, the barber of the title, who by the end of the opera has become the factotum of the Count Almaviva, is a valet figure in the Harlequin mould, endowed with all the cunning and eloquence of his *commedia dell'arte* original. He has an answer to everything—except his own family troubles.

It was not Rossini's way to spend much time on sketches, revisions or adjustments. Nearly everything he composed was ready to be performed, or printed, the moment it left his pen. His recipe for writing an overture to an opera was: "Wait until the eve of the performance. Nothing stimulates the inspiration more than sheer necessity, the presence of a copyist who is waiting for your work, and the insistence of a frantic impresario who is tearing out his hair by the handful."

One desperate opera impresario locked Rossini into a room with a plate of spaghetti and swore not to let him out until he had completed the overture to *Otello*. The overture to *Count Ory* was composed while Rossini was fishing, with his feet in the water. "With the *Barber*. . . I did not compose an overture at all, but took the one intended for the opera *Elizabetta*. The public was quite satisfied." He wrote the overture to *The Thieving Magpie* on the day of the premiere in a room under the eaves of Milan's opera house, La Scala. "I was guarded by four stagehands, who had instructions to throw my manuscript out of the window page by page—down to the copyists who were waiting below to transcribe it."

Two of Rossini's immediate successors, Vincenzo Bellini and Gaetano Donizetti, focused their efforts on the melodies in their operas, in order to give virtuoso singers the opportunity for dazzling technical displays. But in the mid-19th century, Giuseppe Verdi took opera into another psychological dimension: in the dramatic intensity of his music he "crossed the frontier line which it is impossible to define, but beyond which beauty dwells", as the Russian novelist Ivan Turgenev once wrote about a Venetian performance of Verdi's *La Traviata*.

Verdi was to become the living embodiment of the Risorgimento: in shouting *Viva Verdi!*, crowds of patriotic opera-goers could also express their covert loyalty to the king who they expected to bring about the reunification of their country, *Vittorio Emanuele, Re d'Italia*. At the same time, Verdi's

music touched a singularly responsive chord in the Italian imagination. Turgenev reported that *La Traviata* left the performers as spellbound as the audience. The singer playing the heroine who dies of consumption in the final moment of the opera had "tears of joy and real suffering in her eyes. . . her face became transformed, and as the grim phantom of rapidly approaching death confronted her, the words—'*morir sì*

giovane!' (to die so young!)—were torn from her in a prayer of such passionate appeal to divine mercy that the whole theatre shook with frenzied applause and rapturous cries."

After Verdi's string of successes with such heroic subjects as *Rigoletto*, *Aida* and *Otello*, it remained for Giacomo Puccini to round out the great tradition with turn-of-the century operas such as *La Bohème* and *Tosca*. His plots acquired the label *verismo*—realism—because

here were not kings, dukes and generals, but artists, peasants and bohemians, performing passionate actions that were taken, more or less, from real life rather than storybooks.

Puccini's incessant search for new theatrical effects and unusual settings led him to Japan, for *Madame Butterfly*, to China, for *Turandot*, and even to the American frontier, for *La fanciulla del west* (The Girl of the Golden West), an opera whose heroes and villains are singing cowboys and whose heroine is a sort of Annie Oakley; Puccini even experimented with the idea of having eight or 10 horses onstage.

This was the furthest limit to which realism was pushed in Italian opera, and it was not a great success; *La fanciulla del west* almost disappeared from the repertoire after its premiere in 1910. Since then, no composer of Puccini's stature, realist or otherwise, has

Waiting for Puccini's *Turandot* to begin, the audience at Verona's amphitheatre hold lighted candles that outshine the night sky. Spectacular productions in the acoustically perfect Roman arena attract international artists to a summer season of opera and ballet.

emerged to contribute to the genre.

But the operatic tradition has remained very much alive in Italy, thanks in part to the crop of first-rate singers that each generation produces. The Neapolitan tenor Enrico Caruso (1873–1921) possessed one of the most beautiful voices that the opera world has ever known. Luciano Pavarotti, Mirella Freni and Katia Ricciarelli are among today's stars. When promising voices have served their apprenticeship in the provincial opera houses, they go on to bigger and better things abroad, returning for frequent performances at what has remained the very shrine and stronghold of Italian opera—the theatre of La Scala, Milan.

Opera is still a part of popular culture in Italy as nowhere else in the world. Audiences treat singers as if they were football players, cheering and jeering and commenting on their

performance, much as they did in Stendhal's day. Even the smaller cities still have their opera houses. In the summertime, there is opera out of doors—in Verona, Spoleto, Naples, Rome (where the stage is nestled in the ruins of the Roman Baths of Caracalla)—with the night sky adding its lustre to the setting.

While their commitment to opera remains steadfast, modern-day Italian audiences display an equally strong passion for the cinema. Their devotion is understandable: during the past 40 years, many of the nation's best creative talents have expressed themselves on film. In the early post-war years, Italians won international renown with their so-called neo-realist films, portraying the dramas and tragedies of everyday existence. One of the most powerful was Vittorio de Sica's *Bicycle*

Thieves, which related the misadventures that befell an honest working man when his bicycle was stolen.

Other gifted film-makers were drawn to satire and surrealism. Federico Fellini's *La dolce vita* was something of a milestone: it served up what was supposedly a slice of modern Roman life, replete with sex, cynicism and sacrilege—with Anita Ekberg as a voluptuous film star dressed at one point in a monsignore's hat and cassock.

Thereafter Fellini directed a whole series of massive films in which he combined private dreams with apocalyptic commentaries on contemporary society. The most highly praised was $8\frac{1}{2}$, which concerned a director who was unable to choose the subject of his next film. It unfolded at a breathless pace in a succession of dreams, daydreams, memories—many abounding in visual satire that might easily have fitted into a *commedia dell'arte*. The title itself holds up a mirror to Fellini's dilemma in making the film. The director originally adopted it as a sort of opus number: he had shot seven and a half films before that, and could not think of any better name for his latest work.

Luchino Visconti began his film-directing career as a neo-realist, but eventually opted for the gorgeously costumed world of the historical past. His finest films include *Il Gattopardo (The Leopard)*, based on Giuseppe Tomasi di Lampedusa's novel about an aristocratic family coming to terms with the new order in Risorgimento Sicily, and a glittering, moody adaptation of Thomas Mann's *Death in Venice*.

Among the other distinguished Italian film-makers of recent years are Michelangelo Antonioni and Bernardo Bertolucci. Antonioni's film *Blow-Up* took a telescopic and wide-angle view of the fascinating world of the modern British fashion photographer: the intricate plot unwound to the accompaniment of hectic action and sexual fireworks. Bertolucci made his reputation with *Last Tango in Paris*, a film that exploited the autumnal talents of Marlon Brando as an ageing American caught in a web of passion with a clinically detached young Frenchwoman.

Last Tango in Paris is shot through with the qualities that epitomize the best Italian films—visual splendour and psychological acuteness. Whether they deal with aspects of political history or the convolutions of the human psyche, Italian film-directors tend to look at life with the broad sweep of men and women who have grown up alongside real Roman temples and not the papier-mâché kind.

The Italian cinema has also produced a spate of memorable actresses.

Gina Lollobrigida emerged as the first of the post-war European sex-symbols, to be followed soon afterwards by Sophia Loren, who was voted the world's most popular female star in 1969. The tradition of the Italian golden girl has since been upheld by Ornella Muti, among others. Among male stars, no Italian name ranks higher than Marcello Mastroianni's, though some of the younger male leads, notably Ugo Tognazzi, have made themselves an international reputation.

The majority of Italian films are shot for internal consumption and remain unknown to the rest of the world. They deal with Italian themes—the lives of Mamma and Papa, provincial heartbreak romances, and so on—in ways that are more compelling and intelligible at home than abroad. Not even Sophia Loren's persuasive presence managed to make most of her Italian

films exportable to the rest of Europe and the United States.

Italy's visual felicities, on the other hand, are appreciated by the whole of the Western world. As Stendhal said, Italy is a land where "the physical sensation of beauty is wafted at you from every side, like puffs of wind". Generations of its people, using their innate gifts for visual impact and theatrical display, have enhanced nature's handiwork with their own creations.

The Greek colonists in the south selected superb sites for their temples of golden stone. The ruins of Selinunte, in Sicily, provide a case in point: the massive Doric temple dominates a headland that affords a panoramic view of the sea.

While carrying on many of the Greek architectural traditions, the Romans developed a novel style of their own

4

using monumental vaults and domes. Rome is full of great public buildings—temples, theatres, triumphal arches—which they raised to testify to their glory. After the Roman Empire vanished, its buildings remained as a challenge and inspiration to the centuries that followed.

Gradually, the arts of the ancient Roman world were adapted to suit the requirements of medieval Italy. The Romans had decorated their villas at Pompeii and Herculaneum with mythological idylls or with scenes from their favourite plays. Medieval builders adorned their churches with glittering mosaics of the saints and the godhead, or they covered the walls with frescoes. The tradition of painting churches with the stories of the saints to which they were dedicated provided cities and towns the length and breadth of the country with their own treasure-houses of ecclesiastical art.

But towards the end of the medieval period, paintings in this tradition lost their conviction and power; their perpetrators were content to follow the old formulae mechanically, without any feeling for the subject. As a reaction against this decline, the artists of the wealthy cloth-merchants' city of Florence began as early as the 13th century to rethink their aims and methods; in the process, they inaugurated that astonishingly fruitful epoch in the history of art, the Renaissance.

To imitate nature, and even to improve on it, was the aspiration of the Florentine innovators, and their central concern was to create a new image of man. To this end, they studied human anatomy, the science of optics and the laws of perspective. They also turned for inspiration to the classical art of Greece and Rome—works that were never quite forgotten but for centuries had been virtually ignored. In the heroic proportions and poses of the ancient statues, Renaissance artists recognized the idealized human being, the improvement on nature. Psychological truth mattered to them as much as convincing forms, and in their portrayal of human emotions and interactions these artists surpassed anything in the classical canon.

In the early Florentine Renaissance of the 14th and 15th centuries, sculpture held pride of place among the arts—understandably enough, since an object modelled in the round seems closer to nature than a flat, painted surface. One of the greatest sculptors of his day was Lorenzo Ghiberti (1378–1455), who devoted the better part of his life to creating two pairs of monumental bronze doors—"compositions rich with many figures"—for the baptistry of Florence cathedral. Ghiberti was a passionate collector of Roman antiquities. He took his techniques from the Romans: they had developed bronze sculpture into a major art, but in the intervening centuries it had almost fallen into disuse. Ghiberti borrowed many of his motifs, too, from pagan sources, but he adapted them to biblical subject matter and suffused his work with the Christian spirit. A century late, Michelangelo said that Ghiberti's second set of doors was worthy to stand at the gates of paradise.

Michelangelo's own creations were influenced not only by all that had gone before him in the Renaissance but also by new archaeological finds. During his lifetime, from 1475 to 1564, the art collections of the popes were constantly being enlarged by ancient masterpieces such as the massive *Laocoon*, unearthed near the baths of Titus in 1506. Created by Greek sculptors of the first century B.C., the *Laocoon* group depicts the legendary priest of Apollo who, with his sons, is attacked by serpents as punishment for disobeying the commands of the god.

Michelangelo's subsequent work was powerfully influenced by *Laocoon*'s dramatic theme of human suffering, expressed in histrionic gestures of despair. He applied the same theatricality to sculptures such as *The Struggling Captive*, and to his most famous paintings of biblical subjects, the ceiling of the Vatican's Sistine Chapel and its breathtaking companion-piece, *The Last Judgement*.

All three of the foremost artists of the High Renaissance—Leonardo da Vinci, Michelangelo and Raphael—were vitally interested in the problem of how to express human character in art. Da Vinci was determined to "paint the face in such a way that it will be easy to understand what is going on in the mind". When he created his great mural of the *Last Supper* in Milan, he focused on the differing reactions of the 12 disciples at the dramatic moment when Christ announces that one of them is about to betray him. Raphael, the youngest of the three artists, was master of the large-scale narrative

4

composition, but also possessed an extraordinary gift for portraiture.

Expressiveness remained one of the hallmarks of Italian art during the centuries that followed the High Renaissance, when both the subjects and their treatment became increasingly melodramatic. By their flamboyant use of light and shade, late 16th-century painters such as Caravaggio depicted scenes from the lives of the saints as though they were taking place onstage under theatrical lighting. A German critic, Johann Mattheson, remarked in 1728, towards the end of the baroque era, that "the whole world has become a giant theatre", and it was the Italians who led the way, not just in painting but also in the exuberant design of their churches and palaces.

In Rome, the High Baroque is exemplified by the work of Gianlorenzo Bernini, the prodigious 17th-century architect and sculptor who left a stronger imprint on the city than any other individual artist. Rome is replete with monuments, loggias and ornamental sculpture created by Bernini, with churches, chapels, altars and tombs designed by Bernini, with bridges, courtyards and façades decorated by Bernini. The two immense semicircular colonnades in front of the great basilica of St. Peter's are Bernini's handiwork, as are many of the most striking details in St. Peter's itself, including the massive bronze canopy over the main altar, which is supported on corkscrew-twisted columns.

Southern Italy provided another fertile seedbed for baroque sculpture and painting. Here, an extravagant realism held sway: the villa of the Prince of Palagonia, near Palermo, was guarded in the 18th century by six colossal statues of halberdiers and approached along a vast avenue flanked by sculpted monsters. For a landscape garden in Caserta, near Naples, the 18th-century sculptor Vanvitelli created a life-size tableau depicting the legendary hunter Actaeon's encounter with the goddess Diana and her entourage. Clusters of elegant marble figures seem to move freely against a background of rocks and cascading water.

Meanwhile, in the north-east, the artists of Venice had developed a distinct school of their own. Never as intellectual as the Florentines in their approach to painting, the Venetians of the 15th and 16th centuries beguiled the eye with their rich harmonies of colour, the romantic landscapes in which their compositions are set, and the element of mystery that suffuses their works. Titian was the greatest artist among them; he drew upon the example of his predecessors Bellini and Giorgione, and in his turn provided inspiration for Veronese and Tintoretto. After a lull in the 17th century, the 18th century witnessed another flowering of Venetian art. Tiepolo decorated ceilings with a rococo lightness of touch and dizzy use of foreshortening; Canaletto's topographical pictures look almost like stage sets.

For a while, Italian art seemed to mark time while the nation preoccupied itself with the turbulent political events of the 19th century. But at the beginning of the 20th century, the members of a new movement, who called themselves "Futurists", played a significant part in preparing Europe for the advent of modern art. The Futurists were the most theatrical art-revolutionaries of the day. Beginning in 1909, their ideological leader Filippo Marinetti created an incendiary new vocabulary with his manifestos. "A racing car whose hood is adorned with great pipes… is more beautiful than the *Victory of Samothrace*," he proclaimed. His audiences were indignant at the belittling of the sculpture of the Greeks, but Marinetti pressed on unabashed. Museums were "cemeteries" and it was time to tear them down. "Turn aside the canals to flood the museums! Oh, the joy of seeing the glorious old canvases bobbing adrift on those waters, discoloured and shredded!"

Of course, most of this was merely clever propaganda, taken seriously only by the nihilist fringe that afterwards followed Mussolini. In point of fact Marinetti's artist-disciples—men like Carrá, Balla and Severini—produced a fascinating body of Futurist art that now hangs peaceably in the museums alongside the heritage from earlier centuries which Marinetti had previously scorned.

Italy boasts some of the richest museums and galleries in the world, but most of its artistic heritage is to be seen in a more natural context. Paintings still hang in the churches and monasteries that commissioned the artists hundreds of years ago, and famous sculptures adorn working fountains. This is the way the Italians like it—they prefer not to treat their mementoes as exhibits that can only be seen under glass. Their traditional procedure is to incorporate the past into the present by grafting new branches on to the root stock of their civilization.

Just as the characters of the *commedia dell'arte* appear again and again in films and operas, so the architects of the Christian era built on the foundations—or within the walls—of ancient temples. The whole of Rome is dotted with such recycled classical buildings.

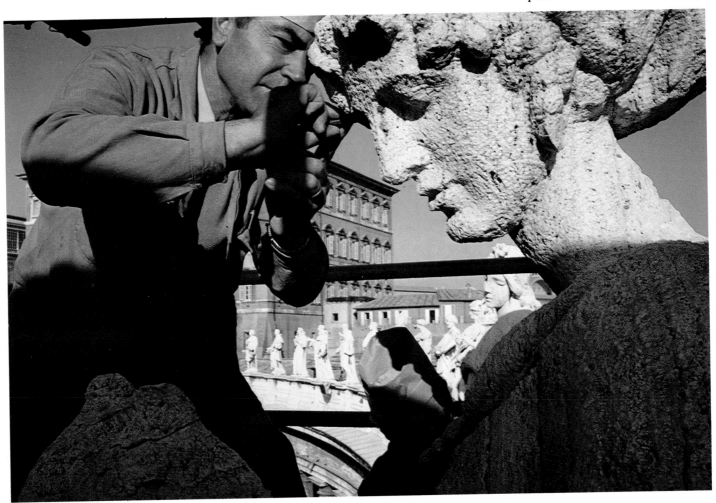

The church of Santa Maria sopra Minerva, for example, is built, as the name reveals, on the remains of a temple of Minerva. The colossal mausoleum of the emperor Hadrian became the Vatican's main fortress, the Castel Sant' Angelo, but now leads yet another existence as a museum—with a restaurant on the battlements.

In the former Theatre of Marcellus, begun by Julius Caesar, is the palace of the Orsini—one of the great aristocratic families of Rome and effectively its rulers during long stretches of the Middle Ages. The Orsini implanted their Renaissance palace above several rows of ancient stone arches: the extra height affords them one of the finest views of the Capitoline hill. A small café, a tobacconist's shop and a shoe wholesaler incongruously now occupy the ground floor of this imposing structure. No-one considers it strange that a princely family should live above a neighbourhood café.

Next door there is the tiny church of Sant' Angelo in Pescheria, wholly encased in what was once the Portico of Octavia—a gift to his sister from Augustus, the first emperor, who liked to boast that he had found Rome a city of bricks and left it a city of marble. The walls of the church consist of Augustus's columns with the spaces between them filled with a stucco-covered mixture of bricks and rubble. During the

4

1980s, one of the Catholic youth movements began to use this church-within-a-monument to celebrate the mass with hand-clapping and shouting accompanied by electric guitars instead of an organ and introducing folk rhythms that were borrowed from American gospel singing. This, too, reflects the Italian genius for adaptation and renewal that has, over the centuries, accounted for the cultural continuity of both church and state.

Historians have pointed out that one reason why the conversion from paganism to Christianity went so smoothly is that the early Christians displayed a remarkable capacity for absorbing and pre-empting existing customs and festivals; for finding something useful in the old formulae that could be applied to new purposes. In art as in religion, however, the new purpose often destroys the old. Much of the marble that was used in the mosaic floors of so many medieval Roman churches, for example, was completely stripped from classical buildings. During the 12th and 13th centuries, whole families of artists and craftsmen specialized in recycling the marble and porphyry of ancient Rome, sawing it into thin sections to produce mosaic floors, columns, thrones, altars, tombs and baldachins. Two exponents of this field, called Cosmas, lent their name to all the others, who became known as Cosmati.

Present-day Italians sometimes appear to accept their artistic heritage as casually and with as little respect as did the Cosmati. They will proudly announce that their cities are the best in the world, but they come near to ruining them with their excessive love of the car, which clogs the narrow medieval streets and chokes the spacious piazza. The shores of the incomparable Bay of

One of Venice's recurrent floods squeezes the crowds crossing St. Mark's Square on to an emergency causeway of planks. In winter, the worst season for *acqua alta* — high water—the city keeps platforms stacked ready in the squares.

Naples are littered with plastic bottles and other flotsam. Paintings in the churches are rarely well tended. During the post-war years, Italian builders ravaged the landscape: speculative construction created high-rise deserts on the outskirts of the most beautiful cities, and much of the finest coastline became a mass of concrete blockhouses. Few voices were raised in protest against this development.

But the problem lies not so much in public indifference as in the scale of the effort that would be required to preserve all of the nation's heritage. Italy possesses a greater concentration of art treasures than any other country, and a colossal programme would be needed to give each one ideal treatment. Isolated case histories reveal that Italians do care about their cultural legacy, and have always done so.

The indefatigable Bernini, for example, once over-reached himself—when he gilded the lily by adding two small bell-towers to the perfect proportions of the domed Pantheon, another of the pagan temples that had been transformed into a Christian church. The people of Rome were very decided in their opinions of Bernini's efforts: they had liked the building better without the additions, which they dubbed "donkey's ears". After two centuries of complaints, the pair of offending bell-towers were pulled down so that the Pantheon could stand once again in all its classical rotundity.

In 20th-century Rome, also, the conservationists find a hearing. The city has preserved the low skyline of its historic centre by means of building regulations and has spent agonizing decades constructing its underground railway system, because the bulldozers keep revealing more archaeological remains which ought to be excavated.

Florence provides a dramatic instance of Italians coming to grips with conservation. Floods in November 1966—when the Arno River burst its banks—caused grievous damage to pictures, sculptures and buildings. Even as the river was rising, the curators and art specialists struggled waist-deep in water to remove threatened paintings from the flooded museums; thanks to their courageous efforts, many important works were saved from destruction. Thousands of other pieces, however, were either destroyed or severely damaged. Yet the rescue operations that continued afterwards were impressive. Italian specialists collaborated with teams of experts sent from other countries, which also raised large sums for the repair of paintings and library archives. The damaged buildings were lovingly restored by local masons and craftsmen.

On the very day that Florence was inundated, Venice suffered the worst floods of its history. The storms that filled the Arno to overflowing also whipped up the Adriatic; Venice was submerged under 2 metres of water. Venice's crisis, unlike Florence's, could not be mitigated by a once-and-for-all conservation effort—for, tragically, the 1966 inundation was only one of many which were rapidly rotting away the fabric of the city. Floods became more and more frequent in the course of the 1960s and early 1970s.

The cause of the watery onslaught was twofold. Because of the shifting of the earth's crust, the sea was rising, meanwhile the islands on which Venice is built were sinking. With their stone houses founded on wooden piles and mud, Venetians have had to cope for centuries with subsidence. The situation, however, deteriorated sharply in the decades after World War II, when industries on the mainland began pumping huge quantities of water from beneath Venice's lagoon, thus lowering the water table and compacting the soil. The same industries also polluted the air with chemicals that gnawed away at Venice's buildings and statues.

In the late 1960s, in the wake of the devastating flood, the world's biggest and most ambitious conservation effort was launched to save Venice. National societies from all over the world set about restoring individual buildings from the ravages of air and water. In the decade that followed, the Italian government virtually halted Venice's submersion by providing a new supply of water for the city and, more importantly, for the mainland industries threatening it. Huge aqueducts were built to carry ample supplies from the rivers that feed the lagoon to the points of use; now that pumping from beneath the lagoon has ceased, the water table has returned to its natural level.

Venice still needs protection, however, from the high tides that immerse it several times a year. Moves to erect flood barriers at the entrances to the lagoon foundered repeatedly against bureaucratic inertia and the violent disagreements of all the experts who were called in to assess the gigantic engineering problems raised. At last, however, work is now under way to build a set of moveable flood barriers. The project will take many years to complete, but there is every reason to believe that science will conspire with politics to preserve this unlikeliest of communities—"a city of rose and white", as the British painter J. M. W. Turner described it, "rising out of an emerald sea against a sky of sapphire blue".

FIGURES IN AN IMMEMORIAL LANDSCAPE

The landscapes and cityscapes of Italy have been indelibly engraved on the Western consciousness through the works of the nation's great artists. The golden age of Italian landscape painting lasted only a few decades, from the mid 15th to the early 16th century. At this time, the scientific currents of the Renaissance were encouraging artists to observe nature and record what they saw. In consequence, the background settings of both religious and secular paintings became increasingly naturalistic. Later, in the High Renaissance of the 16th century, painters rejected the idea of merely reproducing what was before them; they intensified and idealized every element of a picture, including the background.

Today, much of Italy remains as it was when recorded by such Early Renaissance painters as Piero della Francesca and Antonio Pollaiuolo. Travellers can still encounter the cypress-clad slopes of Tuscany, the conical hills of Umbria, the bustling waterways of Venice, which they have seen depicted in the world's galleries.

But the traveller's sense of recognition is in part an illusion, for even in the Early Renaissance, artists were not slavish followers of nature. Rather, they assembled their pictures from different elements, some drawn from life and others from artistic conventions. The illuminated manuscripts of the medieval period provided one source of idealized mountains and lakes, and the works of north European artists such as the van Eycks were also becoming influential in Italy. In the painting on the right by the Venetian artist Giovanni Bellini, for example, the acutely observed castle and fields in the wintry Po valley are set against distant mountains inspired by Flemish models. Bellini has bathed the entire landscape in early morning light, thus blending it into a harmonious whole.

Giovanni Bellini's *Virgin of the Meadow* (1510) contemplates her child in a landscape of harmony and eternal stillness. Bellini was among the first generation of Italian artists to use oil paint, which, with its translucency and rich colour, lent a new verisimilitude to depictions of nature.

Vittore Carpaccio's *Miracle of the Holy Cross* (1494) depicts a crowded scene at the Rialto, Venice's mercantile centre. The wooden bridge was the forerunner of the stone Rialto Bridge, which was built in 1590 and still stands today. The miracle, the curing of a madman, is relegated to the loggia on the left.

In the *Martyrdom of St. Sebastian* (1475) by the Pollaiuolo brothers, the saint suffers at the hands of his tormentors in a landscape reminiscent of the Arno valley near Florence, though the far mountains are imaginary. The arch may symbolize Rome, where Sebastian, a soldier, died for his faith in 288 A.D.

CLARVS INSIGNI VEHITVR TRIVMPHO ·
QVEM PAREM SVMMIS DVCIBVS PERHENNIS ·
FAMA VIRTVTVM CELEBRAT DECENTER ·
SCEPTRA TENENTEM

Piero della Francesca's *Triumph of Federigo da Montefeltro* **(1466) shows the Duke of Urbino and his wife** *(right)* **in**

QVE MODVM REBVS TENVIT SECVNDIS ·
CONIVGIS. MAGNI DECORATA RERVM ·
LAVDE GESTARVM VOLITAT PER ORA ·
CVNCTA VIRORVM ~

allegorical procession through the Umbrian countryside. An inscription on a stone parapet in front describes the event.

In his *Annunciation* (1472), Leonardo da Vinci reproduces the daisies and lilies in the foreground in scientific detail. But he refines the silhouettes of the cypress trees behind the angel into almost geometrically perfect forms— and the mountain is pure fantasy, conveying the unattainable sublime.

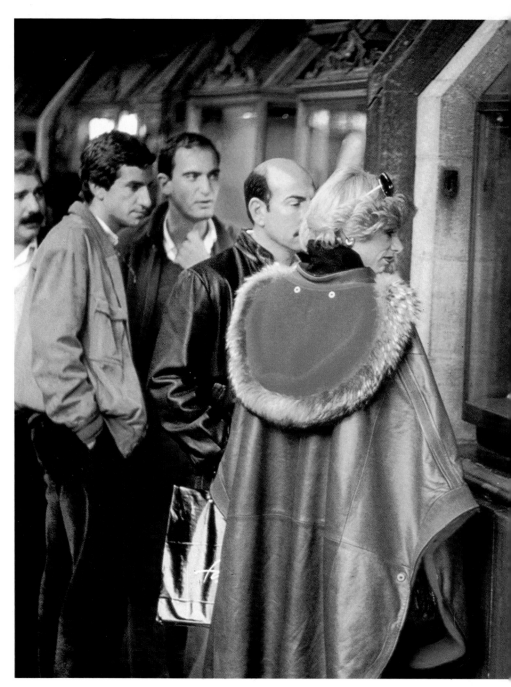

THE EBULLIENT ECONOMY

A visitor to a typical industrial country catches hardly a glimpse of its economy in action; hidden away in industrial parks and office blocks, manufacturing and business remain mere abstractions. But in Italy the economy is tangible: travel around, and you encounter it in every back street. Workshops turn out machine tools, knitwear, jewellery or gloves; markets sell the produce of small cultivators; bars and restaurants appear at every corner. Italy is one of Europe's economic heavyweights, and its gross domestic product is ranked among the world's top seven. Yet with innumerable home industries spilling on to their pavements, parts of Italy's cities have almost the atmosphere of an oriental bazaar.

With the small scale of Italy's most typical ventures goes a pattern of life that other industrial countries have lost. Whereas Americans and northern Europeans like to get their work done briskly or grimly before settling down to leisure and family life, the Italians live their work and involve their families around it. To an outsider their attitude seems carefree, perhaps even lazy: an artisan will interrupt his labours for extended meals, long siestas, vigorous conversation. But the same artisan will be back at his workbench until sunset in the cool evening of the day, and his brothers and cousins will probably be there helping him.

In Italy, there are about a million manufacturing enterprises with an average number of employees of only seven, and many more equally small outfits offering services of one sort or another. These small businesses are the Italian economy's great strength. Families working for themselves are motivated to make a success of their venture; they will cheerfully put in long hours and go without immediate rewards for the sake of tomorrow. Their operations, moreover, are more adaptable than large concerns; with limited stocks and low capital outlays, small-scale entrepreneurs can move in a new direction as soon as they sense a change in the market.

At the opposite extreme of the industrial scale, Italy is the home of some of the world's most famous manufacturing brandnames. Fiat, with an output that exceeds more than a million vehicles each year, is Europe's largest car producer. Olivetti is Europe's most enterprising creator of office equipment. Pirelli is one of Europe's leading tyre-makers. All three firms have international interests.

Giant enterprises and small businesses have, between them, transformed Italy's economy in only four decades. At the end of the Second World War, Italy was a poor agrarian nation without a tradition of trading on a large scale with other countries. Today, Italy exports a higher proportion of its manufactures than any other industrial country except West Germany. The average Italian is twice as rich in real

Elegantly attired in a fur-trimmed leather cape, a woman pauses outside one of Florence's many jewellery shops. With its artistic heritage and its modern boutiques, the city typifies the unbroken tradition of fine design and craftsmanship that is one of the main assets of the Italian economy.

117

5

terms as he was as recently as 1960.

If this were the whole story, Italy would be a promised land, and the millions of Italians who exiled themselves in the years after World War II to escape grinding poverty would be rushing home to earn their fortunes instead of waiting to go back to the old country with their pensions. There are, however, darker aspects to the Italian economy. One of them is the very uneven distribution of the new wealth.

Industry is concentrated in an inverted triangle of territory that stretches between Turin, Venice and Leghorn. Within this area, and indeed throughout the north, people live as well as anywhere in Europe. Below Tuscany and Umbria, Italy is predominantly poor. Milan, the commercial heart of the north, may have outskirts scarred with factories and depressing working-class housing, but the overall impression is of people making a lot of money and cheerfully spending it on anything the world can provide. In contrast, the city of Rome—a mere 60 kilometres south of Umbria—is visibly worse off, though the capital is rich in art and history, and festooned with some fine shopping streets. Expensive stores are more thinly dispersed, and the fabric of the place is less cared for.

Even in the north, however, the normally buoyant economy is liable to capsize into a sudden depression. One reason for its precariousness is Italy's heavy reliance on imported energy. The country has little oil and only low-grade coal. Its resources of gas and hydroelectric power are sufficient to meet just one sixth of its total energy needs. Two thirds of the fuel it uses is imported oil, and imported gas and coal make up a further one sixth of consumption. Continued success at exporting their natural talents in the form of brilliantly designed cars or couture is crucial for the Italians, because it is only by selling abroad that they can afford to pay their colossal fuel import bills. And when world oil prices shoot up, the Italian economy rocks wildly.

Italy looks doomed to continue its dependency on imported oil for many years to come. There has been a move to build more nuclear power stations to boost the tiny proportion of electricity—just over 1 per cent—produced at present by these means, but projects have been slowed by interminable local planning enquiries. A proposed switch to using more imported coal is held up because it would require heavy investment in coal ports and handling facilities at the points of consumption. Some relief is imminent from natural gas imported through an undersea pipeline that has been built between Italy and Algeria. The first supplies of natural gas flowed into the country in 1983, but the new resource did not immediately make a notable difference because local distribution pipelines were in short supply, and oil-burning power stations had yet to be converted to gas.

Another reason why prosperity can never be taken for granted is conveyed in a recurring image of the Italian economy—a champion racehorse laden with an overweight jockey. There is nothing wrong with the beast itself, which is swift and powerful when unhindered. But the unfortunate creature is saddled with an onerous political and social system.

Italy's public sector has been more or less out of control for decades. Politicians use the large state-owned industrial sector left over by the Fascists as a machine for delivering votes through the construction of factories in depressed areas. The state-owned companies lose some 3 billion dollars a year because they employ too many people to make goods that nobody wants at their prices and qualities. Financial management of essential public services, such as hospitals and schools, is often either inefficient or corrupt, and subject to no clear limits. The government never really knows how much it will end up having to borrow at home or abroad to balance its books at the end of the year.

Not surprisingly, Italy's public sector deficit tops the European league. Total government debt outstanding amounts to more than 80 per cent of a year's output of the whole economy—compared with under 60 per cent in Britain and under 50 per cent in the United States.

Because the state pre-empts so much of the available capital, scarcity pushes up the price of money. Interest rates for loans rise, which makes it more difficult for private businesses to raise funds for growth. Thus the public deficit drives up the cost of doing business, and ultimately the cost of living. At almost any point in time since the mid-1970s, Italian inflation has been the highest among the world's major industrial countries. This in turn increases the cost of exports, making them less competitive in the world marketplace. The only solution is for the Italian lira to fall against other currencies—but that also puts up import prices and notches Italy's inflation up again.

Every few years, sober-suited international bankers and economists from the International Monetary Fund (an organization that lends governmental funds to countries with balance-of-payments problems) feel obliged to descend on Rome and start lecturing

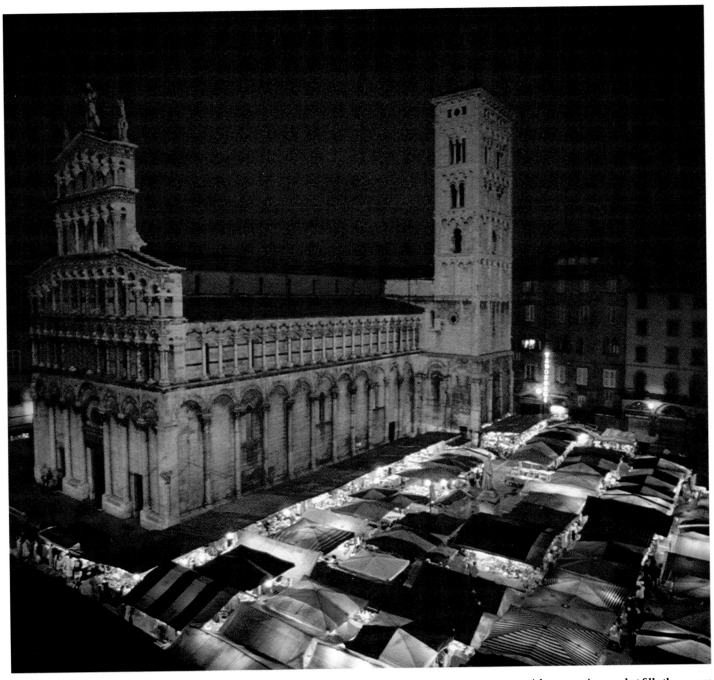

A busy evening market fills the square beside the church of San Michele in the Tuscan town of Lucca. Italy's profusion of street markets, with family-run stalls offering a small range of goods, explains why it has the highest number of retailers in Europe—one for every 60 people.

A CITY'S TRADITION OF VIOLIN CRAFTSMANSHIP

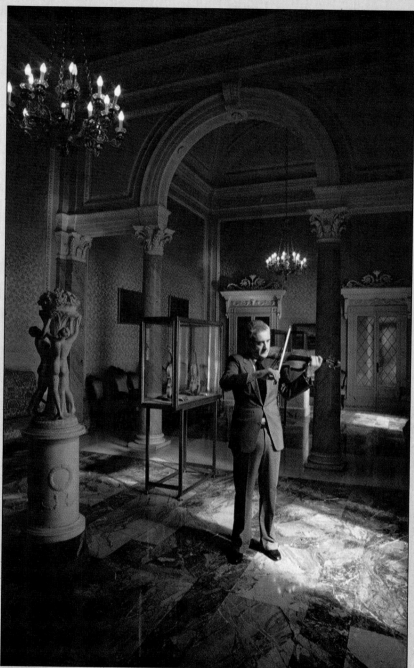

The curator of the violin collection in Cremona's city hall plays one of the instruments.

The ancient town of Cremona in Lombardy has a special place in musical history. Between the 16th and the 18th centuries, the finest violins the world has ever known were created in the city's workshops. Here, Andrea and Nicola Amati, Giuseppe Guarneri and the master of masters, Antonio Stradivari, made instruments of such miraculous tone that even today they are the choice of the great virtuosi. Some examples of the old violin-makers' art are housed in Cremona's city hall, and every morning one or two are played so that they retain the qualities built into them centuries ago.

But Cremona is not merely a repository of past glories. Tucked away in a warren of medieval streets are the ateliers of over 50 master-builders, some of whom teach their esoteric craft to students from more than 20 countries. Striving to reproduce the perfection of past eras, they take pains with every detail of the complex construction process.

Each violin is composed of 72 pieces of wood of at least seven types—chiefly maple, for the hard back and neck of the instrument, and spruce, for the soft front. The wood is first aged for up to 10 years, in which time it dries slowly and evenly. After the lengthy work of cutting and gluing, the newly formed violins are then seasoned for a further year.

The final stage in a violin's creation—one vitally important for its timbre—is the application of some 30 layers of varnish. Each coat dries in the open air, and one of the characteristic sights of Cremona is lines of violins hanging above the workshop roofs like washing. The master-builders who use the most traditional methods average five to six violins a year, of which 90 per cent are exported at around $10,000 each.

Stradivari is immortalized in stone.

After applying glue, a craftsman clamps the body of a violin.

Varnish dries on violins hanging among Cremona's rooftops. Below, blocks of wood are propped against a parapet to season.

5

Italians and their politicians about living beyond their national means. When things get really bad, the Bank of Italy takes drastic measures. It slams the brakes on the economy by reducing the supply of money and credit available either to the government or to the private sector. The whole system slows down to a crawl until debts, price rises and the gap between exports and imports all decline to more reasonable proportions. These periods of painful readjustment rarely seem to coincide with the recessions of the world's other industrialized countries, nor do Italy's bursts of exhilarating progress always coincide with boom years elsewhere. With its peculiar strengths and weaknesses, the Italian economy behaves like no other.

Both the strengths and the weaknesses have roots that extend far into the past. Since the war, the strengths have far outweighed the weaknesses, but previously the opposite was true; for most of the 19th century the obstacles in the way of industrialization seemed prohibitive. Lack of energy sources was even more of a problem than it is in these oil-burning days because the cost of importing coal was prohibitively high. The political situation, moreover, discouraged any risk-taking. Centuries of foreign domination followed by the disturbances of the Risorgimento left the Italians with a strong preference for unadventurous investment in property and land. And, before unification, any entrepreneur would have found it hard to sell his goods in Italy since there was no nationwide market; even afterwards, much of the population was too poor to buy industrial products.

On the other hand, Italy's human resources constituted a strength which would eventually enable these handicaps to be overcome. Many peasants were part-time artisans who could draw upon a long tradition of fine design and craftsmanship. Silk manufacture was a widespread cottage industry, producing one of Italy's main exports. In Venice, glassmaking skills that had developed over hundreds of years were still carefully nurtured.

Italians were also familiar with trade and finance. Venice and Genoa had for centuries been among the foremost ports of the Mediterranean, and the Italian merchant fleet in the 19th century was one of Europe's largest. Italians had invented banking in the 12th century, and by the 19th century had built up an extensive network of local finance houses. Italy also produced several distinguished scientists and inventors in the 19th and early 20th centuries—among them Alessandro Volta, who made the first electric battery, and Guglielmo Marconi, who developed radio telegraphy.

From the 1870s onwards, these varied talents began to be channelled into industry. Giovanni Pirelli built his first rubber-processing factory in Milan in 1872. The Olivetti enterprise dates from 1908, when the enlightened Camillo Olivetti sited a typewriter factory at Ivrea in the healthy air of the Piedmont hills, and founded a model community on the outskirts of the town to house his workers.

In 1899, a group of industrialists led by Giovanni Agnelli, a former cavalry officer, created Fabbrica Italiana Automobili Torino—Fiat for short. By 1914 Fiat was producing more than 3,000 cars a year, and a clutch of other car manufacturers—Alfa Romeo, Lancia and Bianchi among them—had also made an international name for their engineering and stylish design. Italy gradually became more prosperous, though it continued to lag behind the industrial giants of the day—Britain, Germany and the United States.

Industry was taking root only in the north of the country—indeed, most of it was concentrated round Milan, Turin and Genoa. The south proved to be more resistant to accepting any kind of change. It suffered from its position on the periphery of Europe; new ideas were slow to filter southwards, export markets were hundreds of kilometres away. The skills widespread in the north were lacking. Unification of Italy exacerbated the inherent weaknesses of the south by opening it up to competition with the north. The relative poverty of the south today is no accident: it is the almost inevitable consequence of geography and history.

Mussolini became head of government in 1922. He was initially in favour of free trade, but after a few years he declared *laissez-faire* economics to be out of date, and set up a bureaucracy that intervened at every level in industry—and severely hampered its efficiency. In 1933, after several bank collapses, Mussolini created the Institute for Industrial Reconstruction (IRI), whose function was to lend money to firms in difficulty. Initially IRI's role was simply to restore ailing companies to health. But close supervision of industry corresponded with Mussolini's economic ideas, and soon IRI became a permanent shareholder in the enterprises it bailed out. The result was that by 1939, the state, through IRI, controlled many of Italy's leading firms, especially in the steel, engineering, shipbuilding and banking sectors.

Mussolini also attempted to direct agriculture, but with unfortunate re-

The chimneys of a geothermal power station dominate a Tuscan hillside. Italy's volcanic geology traps steam in porous rocks about a kilometre below ground. Extracted through pipes, the steam generates enough electricity to meet 1 per cent of Italy's energy needs.

sults. Coaxing a living out of Italy's poor land had always been a struggle, and investment was rarely high enough to realize even the limited potential of the soil. The best results were obtained by the growers of olives, vines and fruit trees—crops which flourished even where rainfall was scanty and fields rocky. Instead of acknowledging this fact, however, Mussolini attempted to gain agricultural self-sufficiency by waging a "battle for grain". Wheat production was duly increased, but only by growing the cereal on land manifestly unsuitable for it—land where other crops would have fared better. The miseries of the countryside were exacerbated in the 1930s when Mussolini, fearing social unrest among the growing class of industrial workers, forbade any further movement from the country to the cities. As the New World countries imposed quotas on immigrants, cutting off the traditional escape route of the Italian peasant, more and more people became trapped in rural poverty.

After the war, when Italy set itself the task of industrializing rapidly, this particular problem transformed itself into a boon. In contrast to such countries as France and West Germany, Italy had an enormous potential labour force on its own peasant plots. The post-war generation that came off the fields was prepared to work for low wages, and it was docile. More and more factory workers were joining one of the trade unions, all of which had political affiliations. The largest union grouping was linked to the Communist and Socialist parties, the second to the Christian Democrat party, and the third to several of the small political parties. However, ideological differences between the three camps sapped

123

5

the coercive power of the trade unions.

No other country could boast both an enormous untapped labour force and the inventive skills that Italy had already demonstrated. Shrewdly assessing his nation's potential just after the end of World War II, Vittorio Valletta, the president of Fiat, described Italy as the "engineering granary of Europe". Within a very few years, Italy was bearing out his claim.

Italy's economic miracle lasted from 1945 to the late 1960s. In the early years, the economy received a tremendous boost in the form of foreign aid—first from the Anglo-American invasion forces and, after 1948, from the United States government, which provided funds, industrial equipment and know-how under the Marshall Plan.

By the start of the 1950s, the Italian economy was growing at a rate of more than 5 per cent, and the nation managed to sustain that hectic pace throughout the next two decades. Most of Italy's growth was to be found in medium-technology manufacturing—cars, domestic appliances and plastics—but civil engineering and tourism also loomed large.

In France and Japan, the only other populous countries to rival Italy's growth during these years, the direction of industrial development was determined by the central government. Italy's economic miracle had nobody in charge—and Italians were well aware that in their country the government was more likely to be a hindrance than a help. Being such a recent federation of states, and lacking France's tradition of centralization or West Germany's cohesion, Italy was not equipped to run a centrally planned economy. Mussolini's efforts in that direction had been unsuccessful, and it soon became apparent that post-war governments would be little better suited to the task. Short-lived coalitions quickly became the norm, and patronage and corruption were rife.

However, Italian industry could not launch itself without some state help. The sums of money required for capital investment were huge by any standard, and at the end of the Second World War Italy's financial system was so shaky that only the state could possibly commandeer the necessary credit. One of the great Italian achievements of this period was to devise a means by which industry could benefit from state resources without being damaged by government meddling.

Paradoxically, the principal organ to succeed in keeping state-backed firms at arm's length from politicians was the one created by Mussolini for controlling industry—IRI. The agency was revived and given the task by government of developing basic heavy industries. IRI and various subsidiaries it spawned duly founded modern steel, chemicals and engineering enterprises. The state-backed industries were never entirely free from ministerial pressure, but for a number of years this remained at a very tolerable level. A similar body, the National Hydrocarbons Board (ENI), was established in 1953 to exploit Italy's natural gas supplies. It subsequently branched out into oil refining and the manufacturing of petroleum products. Later, the government created additional holding companies with responsibility for particular industrial sectors.

Italy's lack of industrial infrastructure, which had looked to some like a disadvantage, quickly revealed itself to be a blessing. Building heavy industry from scratch, Italy was able to follow the same virtuous circle that Japan

124

traced during the post-war period. The state-backed steel industry was developed in parallel with the privately run consumer durables sectors, which were its biggest customers. The efficient steelmakers gave an enormous advantage to the producers of cars and refrigerators, who began to flood Europe with their low-price products after Italy helped to set up the European Economic Community (EEC) in 1957. Successful car and appliance makers were in turn a wonderful comfort to the steelmen, who were able to extend and improve their plants without having to worry about an economic return on their investments.

The partnership between public and private companies worked beautifully; for years IRI and the other holding companies were cited throughout Europe as a model of beneficial government intervention in industry.

While IRI protected state enterprises from government, private firms had to devise their own means of avoiding the attentions of politicians—who might otherwise intervene, for example, to insist that a factory be sited in an unsuitable spot as a favour to their constituents. There were two courses a company could take to avoid such unwelcome pressures. One was to shrink so small that it no longer interested politicians. The other was to grow large and powerful enough to be able to flout their wishes. Thus, where economies of scale were not paramount, Italy developed its unique brand of decentralized production—the small firms that are the most striking feature of Italian industry. At the same time, the big companies such as Olivetti and Pirelli grew ever larger.

The biggest private group of all was and continues to be Fiat, which not

Soaring above the skyline of Milan, the commercial centre of modern Italy, the Pirelli tower symbolizes the confidence of the post-war boom years. The giant rubber company built this 32-storey office block in the late 1950s; for more than a decade, it was the tallest such building in Europe.

only dominates car production in Italy but has long since diversified into such areas as mining, finance, newspapers and medical supplies. Italian journals love to run opinion polls on who the readers consider are the most powerful figures in Italy. Giovanni Agnelli, the leader of the family that still owns most of the shares in the Fiat empire founded by his grandfather, always figures in the top few.

The immense influence of Fiat has not only cushioned the company from political interference but also gained it some special privileges, notably long-term restrictions on the import of Japanese cars. The arrangement was a reciprocal one, and had first been suggested in the 1950s by the Japanese, who were alarmed at the prospect of a flood of Italian car imports damaging their infant automobile industry. But even after Japanese car manufacturing had reached maturity, the agreement between the two countries remained in force, and contributed to Fiat's phenomenal growth. Graceful Turin became increasingly dominated by the motor works in its suburbs.

Though Turin and Fiat eventually became almost synonymous to most Italians, the city also exemplifies the opposite pole of the nation's industry. In the 1960s, while Fiat itself was growing, a vast hinterland of engineering workshops—employing as many people as the car works themselves—spread in and around the city in order to supply the factory. And in other cities throughout Italy similar developments were taking place.

During the 1950s, import duties in force since the 1930s were gradually removed from such products as textiles, clothing, leather, jewellery and ceramics. The resulting international

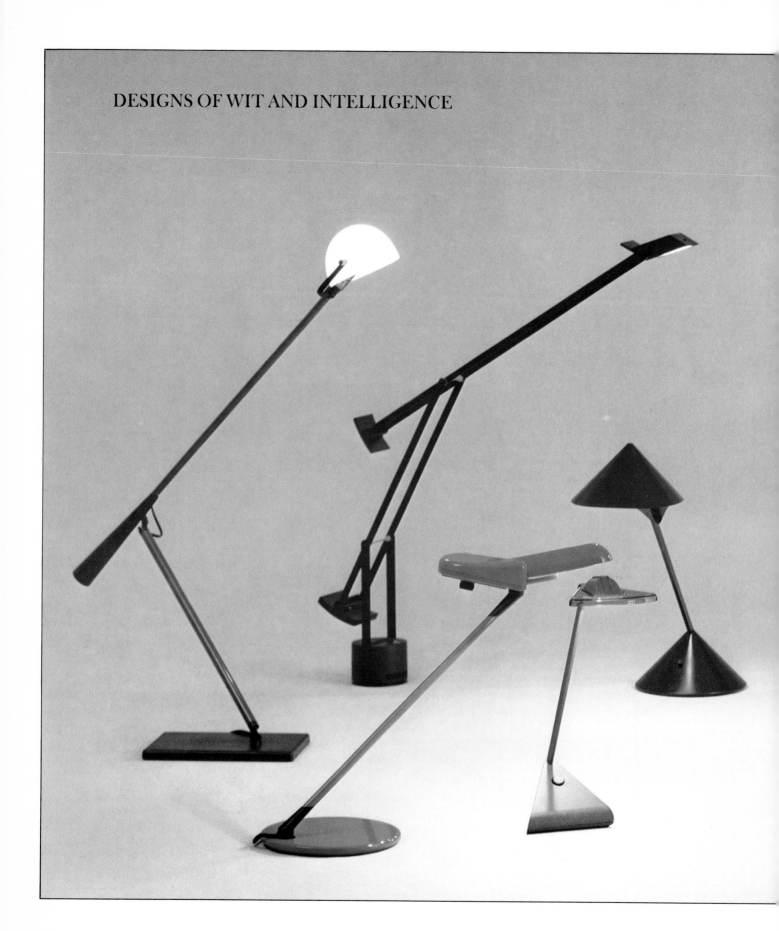

Italian mass-produced goods are renowned worldwide for their formal beauty, their brilliant colouring and their innovative solutions to functional problems. The Italian flair for design touches products as diverse as typewriters, sports cars and ballpoint pens, but it is in furnishings and fittings that it has made the greatest impact.

It was immediately after World War II that Italy started to make a name as a fount of fresh design ideas.

Many of the best designers of the 1950s and 1960s had trained as architects. Opportunities to create interesting buildings were few because of a shortage of capital, so they directed their talents towards the shaping of consumer goods and interiors. They established a pattern of working which endures: designers work in independent groups, offering their services to a range of companies. Freed from worries over management and sales, the

groups—many based in Milan— can concentrate on aesthetics.

From the start, the design groups embraced high technology and new materials: indeed, sleek creations in moulded plastic epitomize the Italian style. Synthetics are invariably used for their own sake, not disguised as wood or stone. The futuristic table lamps grouped here realize the potential of metal, plastic and the latest technology with typically Italian panache.

5

competition was a sharply effective, if rather painful, stimulus to small Italian producers of these goods. The family businesses competed but they also co-operated with each other. Sometimes they would even contract work out to rivals with spare capacity; often they would club their resources together to launch collective marketing and advertising campaigns. Whether their output was luxury items or more modest products, these small producers were rarely content with their easily accessible local markets; they reached out to sell to Europe.

The economic success story of the 1950s and 1960s was marred only by the failure of large-scale industry to take root in the south of Italy. In 1950,

a special bureau called the *Cassa per il Mezzogiorno*, had been set up to finance development in Italy's problem regions. However, most of the organization's huge funds were spent on engineering projects such as motorways and dams, which, though valuable, did not produce long-term employment and mainly benefited the engineering companies from the north that had won the contracts.

Few private manufacturers were keen to build factories in potentially difficult areas. At the government's insistence, some of the state industries were located in the southern regions, notably Europe's largest steelworks at Taranto in Puglia. This massive, integrated seaside complex took in iron ore

that was shipped economically across the world in bulk carriers, then turned out the steel needed by the car and appliance factories in the north. But such a factory hardly touched the problem of rural employment. Built with state capital almost regardless of cost, it was so mechanized that it required only a small work force.

Had it been more labour intensive, it probably would have had the sort of troubles experienced by the state-owned Alfa Romeo company when it set up its Alfasud factory outside Naples. The factory was dogged by frequent strikes, high absenteeism and low-quality finishing because the workers had no tradition of the disciplines of industrial life. The distance

128

from the factory to its markets added high transport charges to the high production costs, and therefore increased the company's difficulties. With time, many of Alfasud's problems were solved, but the long struggle discouraged other companies from following in its footsteps.

Some southern cities, such as Naples, developed their own networks of small businesses to rival those of the north. But these activities were not enough to mop up all the surplus labour, and many southerners had little choice but to leave their homes in search of work. In the 1950s and 1960s about three million went to other EEC countries; several times that number chose to travel to the other end of Italy to work in the thriving factories of the north. Unlike the southerners who remained at home, the migrants adjusted to the demands of the production line and they worked as well as the native northerners. But they did not integrate easily into the social fabric of the new environment. The local inhabitants shunned them, and the southerners' sense of alienation was increased by cramped and poor accommodation.

While the southern migrants had special grievances, other factory workers were getting restive too. They could sense the vigorous momentum of the economy, and yet their pay packets remained slim. Whereas the first generation of industrial workers had been acquiescent employees, their children—who were beginning to enter the work force—began to demand a larger share of the spoils for themselves. The age when Italy could rely on a docile labour force was over.

New trends in factory building reflected the difficult times. Suddenly, instead of giant operations, medium-sized plants accommodating about 700 workers were in vogue. The size limit was calculated so that managers could know most of the employees by name, which presumably would help to improve relations with an increasingly hostile work force. The medium-sized firms did largely succeed in avoiding trouble—but meanwhile, in the massive older firms, discontent increased. Left-wing extremists infiltrated many of the factories to apply their college-learned socialist theories by educating the masses in the exploitative nature of the capitalist system.

The workers' resentments eventually came to a head in the so-called "hot autumn" of 1969, when strikes and demonstrations paralysed much of Italian industry for about a month. After a while, the employers gave way to the workers' demands and conceded unusually large wage increases. The following year, a new law—the "Workers' Charter"—was passed which gave employees increased security in their jobs and spelled out the rights of trade unions within companies.

Their credibility boosted by these successes, the left-wing extremists in the trade unions set about creating anarchy in Italian factories. Over and over again, on the smallest of pretexts and without warning, small groups of workers staged brief stoppages in the big car and engineering plants. The chaos caused by the workers' unpredictable behaviour damaged Italian industry far more than the extra costs incurred by management in granting improved pay and conditions.

In 1973 and 1974, a different crisis came to try Italian industry—the quintupling of oil prices in a matter of months as a result of decisions made by the OPEC producers' cartel. The price rise put a spoke in the wheels of even the best balanced Western economies, and Italy, so dependent on energy imports, suffered more severely than most others. The annual inflation rate rose to 25 per cent.

After four years of doing battle in the factories, the unions found themselves in a formidable position to protect their purchasing power when inflation took off. They won real wage rises of about 10 per cent in 1974 to 1975, and productivity stopped growing.

Next, taking advantage of the vote-buying climate that prevailed in Italian politics, the unions succeeded in pushing through changes in the law that had the effect of more or less institutionalizing inflation. Since 1957, Italian workers had been partly sheltered from the falling value of money by a so-called "moving staircase", which automatically raised their wages as prices rose. But in 1975, the unions managed to greatly extend their protection. All workers, regardless of their earnings, thenceforth received a flat fee that automatically compensated them for as much as 75 per cent of the previous three months' price rises. In practice, this meant that money wages went up even faster than the cost of living, because the better-paid groups fought for extra sums to maintain their differentials, and because various industries negotiated national and local wage deals in addition to the increments that everyone received.

Other European countries that tied wages to the cost of living during the 1970s were able to loosen the linkage by the end of the decade. But Italy had to wait until 1983 for the indexation to be tackled by a government willing to endure unpopularity with the trade

Regimented rows of umbrellas crowd an Adriatic beach at the height of the three-month summer season. Since the 19th century, foreigners have flocked to the 500 kilometres of sand along Italy's eastern shore, but today they are outnumbered by native holidaymakers.

5

unions. Even then, they did not shelve the system and introduced modifications instead. Automatic wage indexation was cut by 15 per cent, but the principle remained.

In the 1970s, inflation combined with unrest in the factories to make Italian goods increasingly uncompetitive. Although the Fiat company was still protected from its Japanese rivals by import quotas, Italy's membership of the EEC prevented the nation from keeping out cars from other European countries. Fiat sales dropped considerably until the company retained barely half the home market it had traditionally dominated. In other European countries, Japanese and West German products were ousting Fiat from its position as market leader. Other big private Italian companies suffered a similar fate at home and abroad.

The unaccustomed experience of industrial failure diverted IRI and the other governmental bodies from their true purpose. As Third World countries began to develop heavy industries such as steelmaking, offering fierce competition to Italy's strike-ridden firms, the country should logically have closed down some of its factories and redirected its work force. But governments were under intense pressure not to take such drastic measures, however much sense it made economically. IRI became a convenient channel for drawing taxpayers' money into loss-making industry, so avoiding the political costs of closing down plants and putting people out of work. The agency quickly became discredited.

No end to the problem seemed in sight, and official forecasts for the economy looked more and more bleak. But the official forecasters were concentrating their attention on the ailing industrial giants and forgetting the existence of the back-street economy—the hundreds of thousands of little firms which employed cheap, non-union labour. Conventional wisdom at that time had it that labour-intensive industry was drifting from Europe to the newly industrializing South-East Asian countries and Latin America. But Italy proved that its labour-intensive sector was still capable of competing internationally. In the late 1970s, the nation managed an extraordinary spurt of progress, growing faster between 1977 and 1980 than any other industrial country. The little firms were responsible for this dazzling performance.

But all the known small firms could not account for the level of economic activity in Italy at the time. Something else was going on—a phenomenon that had already been noted, and christened the submerged or "black" economy. A Rome sociologist, Giuseppe de Rita, first drew the public's attention to it in 1971. His social research bureau obtained evidence that the official economic statistics were hopelessly wrong because they failed to record the output of thousands of manufacturing businesses. These enterprises were operating unseen on the margins of the economy, thereby escaping taxes, keeping clear of union interference and avoiding expensive labour regulations. Instead of employees, these concealed businesses used self-employed consultants or home workers.

De Rita subsequently monitored the progress of the hidden sector, coming to the conclusion that it contributed 20 per cent of Italy's economic output in the course of the 1970s. Unofficial economic activity has long existed, of course, in other countries; Italy was unusual because the unofficial sector was so large, and because it was chiefly concerned with making things rather than performing services—for example, cleaning windows or mending cars. Some saw its workings as a brilliant exercise in capitalist adaptation, others as crude commercial exploitation of working people.

At the start of the 1980s, while small companies continued to prosper, giant concerns discovered a new lease of life. But in contrast to the days of the economic miracle, when state industries had been the pace setters, the big private companies now showed the way for the rest of the economy. The turning point from the anarchy of the 1970s came in October 1980, when thousands of Fiat foremen and middle managers marched through the streets of Turin to protest against the latest in a long series of strikes by their fellow workers. The "march of the 40,000", as it became known, symbolized the new mood of co-operation within industry. Workers and employers combined forces to bring about the transformation that quickly followed their action.

At Fiat, the Agnelli family stood back from the day-to-day management and left the field clear for a new breed of technocrats. The company made huge investments in efficient means of production such as robots. Absenteeism among the workers dropped, productivity rose, and the first new model of the 1980s, the Uno, was voted car of the year in 1984 by the European motoring press. The company regained most of the ground it had lost in and outside Italy, and it soared back to regain the number one car-making position in Europe.

Olivetti staged an equally dramatic recovery at about the same time. The

An aqueduct crosses the dry landscape of Basilicata, in southern Italy. In a bid to develop the disadvantaged south, the Italian government has financed the construction of an irrigation network totalling more than 15,000 kilometres.

firm had nearly collapsed in the 1970s, largely because its managers did not notice until very late that the microchip was rendering obsolete the carefully engineered mechanical innards of its electric typewriters. Losses were more than 100 million dollars in 1978 when Carlo de Benedetti, a rich Piedmontese businessman, was brought in to put matters right. He had briefly held a top position with Fiat, but had found the family atmosphere too pervasive. He put in 17 million dollars of his own money to acquire a 20 per cent holding in Olivetti. Benedetti then set about forming partnerships with French, American, Japanese and Canadian companies in order to get back both the

products and the market share that years of neglect by previous management had allowed to slip.

The firm leaped from the age of the typewriter into the modern computerized office, introducing a range of products that included electronic telexes, desk-top computers, word processors and terminals. Not only was this equipment as beautifully designed as people had come to expect of Italian products, but its systems and software were of top quality. The newly revived firm received an accolade in 1983 when the giant American Telephone and Telegraph company, seeking a European partner for its expansion in office electronics, chose Olivetti and bought a

quarter share in the firm.

Similar recoveries were taking place elsewhere in the big private groups, for example among giant textile manufacturers. Italy had constructed the most modern artificial fibre plants in the world in the 1970s, at a time when global overproduction made the investment seem a financial disaster. But after factory closures everywhere—including Italy—in the late 1970s because of slack demand, the up-to-date Italian plants began to reap in the profits. Partly as a result of this success, clothing and textiles have crept up to number two in the table of Italian manufactured exports, behind machinery. Some of the credit for this achieve-

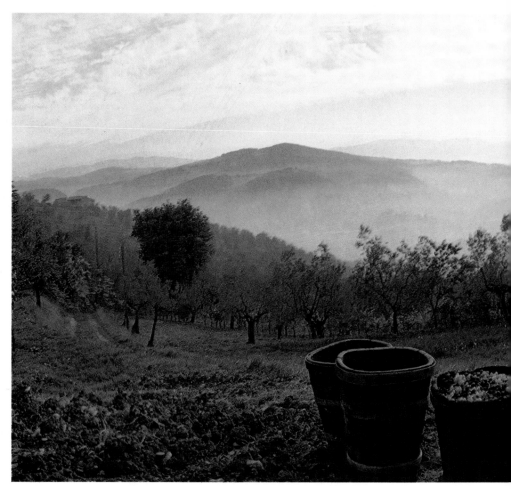

A peasant in Tuscany's Chianti hills crushes grapes that have been partly dried in the sun after picking. Making his family's supply of wine according to local custom, he will add the sugary pulp to the rest of his grapes as they ferment, so as to round out the flavour.

ment, however, must go to the still flourishing tradition of silk manufacture and to the brilliant Italian design houses which, by the early 1980s, had made Milan a serious rival to Paris for the title of world fashion capital.

Another industry that was hit in the 1970s, only to recover in the 1980s, was tourism. In the 1960s, Italy had vigorously sold its sun and its sand—but Spain offered the same attractions at a lower price, and by the 1970s was drawing the crowds away from Italy's beaches. Italy responded to the competition by marketing its unrivalled heritage of art and architecture, locating helpful tourist bureaux in every historic town and signposting itineraries chosen specially for the culturally minded traveller. The results were dramatic. By the early 1980s, tourism was bringing in more foreign currency than any other sector of Italian industry except machinery.

The new strength in the economy sent ripples among the small firms. One sign of health was the emergence of clandestine businesses into the open. Giuseppe de Rita, who had brought the black economy to the attention of the world in 1971, found, a decade later, that in places such as the textile town of Prato near Florence, the number of officially registered workplaces had doubled. De Rita reckoned that the real rate of job creation, though healthy, could not be as high as this, and he concluded that many of the apparently new companies had previously been part of the "black" economy. Some had emerged because they had grown to a point where the increasingly vigilant taxman could spot them, while others appeared simply because the climate for enterprise had improved so much that there was no longer an overwhelm-

ing imperative to remain in hiding.

Only in the traditionally more anarchic south, where the tax inspectors had not yet made much progress, was the submerged economy thought to prevail. Around Naples, for example, millions of pairs of gloves were being turned out each year from an officially tiny number of factories, which could not possibly have been responsible for such a large output.

Though there undoubtedly are hidden pockets of enterprise in the south, the overall southern economy is still as lame as ever. Far from diminishing as a result of all the money poured into southern development in the last few decades, the wealth gap between the

north and the south has actually grown. It is felt all the more because expectations have been aroused by the north's success.

Even in the north, however, there is no room for the workers to become complacent. Agriculture's fortunes have been very mixed. The farming sector had rapidly shed much of its excess work force: in 1960, 6.6 million people worked on the land, and by the mid-1980s this number was reduced to 2.5 million. But the latter figure still amounted to 11 per cent of the total Italian labour force, a much higher percentage than in other industrial countries. Even France, the EEC's other big agricultural employer, had only 8 per cent of its working popula-

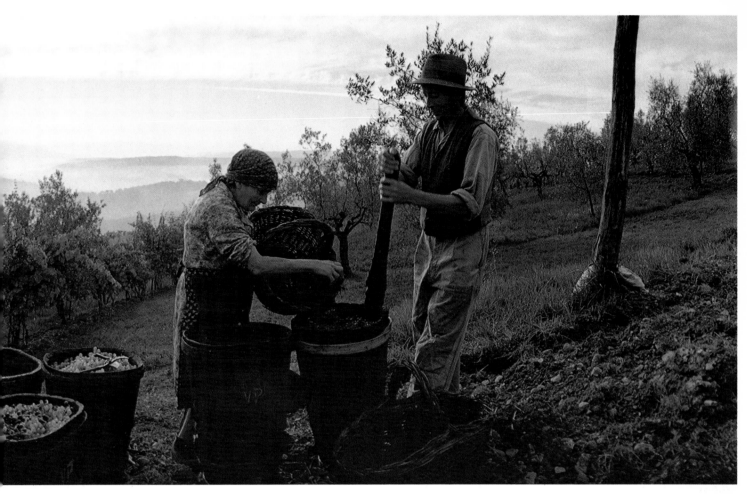

tion on the land in the mid-1980s.

The most efficient Italian farms are comparable with any in Europe. Overall, however, the degree of mechanization is low: Italy has only 46 tractors per 100 workers, for example, compared with nearly twice that in the other large EEC countries. The poor, hilly terrain continues to stand in the way of streamlined methods and large yields. The farming population is ageing fast, and many fear that as the old farmers retire from their struggles with the soil their places will not be taken by members of the younger generation.

The most troubled part of the Italian economy, however, remains the state-owned sector. Losses in this area are still enormous. Painful decisions to close down steelworks have been taken only very reluctantly.

Some of the large private companies have also had a difficult time. Several major kitchen appliance makers almost collapsed in the early 1980s. And their problems point to difficulties that may face a large section of Italian industry. Most economists feel that the straightforward medium-technology manufacturing that played such a big part in the Italian economy of the 1960s is doomed to move to newly industrializing countries. Meanwhile the rich countries will develop high technology production and ever more sophisticated services. To the extent that rich countries do continue to manufacture such goods as refrigerators, they will equip them with sophisticated electronics.

Olivetti excepted, Italian companies have not shown much affinity for complex electronics. The simpler sorts of electronic gadgetry are routinely incorporated in Italian machine tools, but Italians have not kept abreast of the most dazzling innovations. In Italian universities, there are very few chairs of information technology.

The biggest challenge for Italian industry now is to catch up rapidly in these crucial areas. Failure would put the entire engineering sector of Italian manufacturing at risk. But failure is far from inevitable. If the Italians exercise their customary ingenuity, they should look forward to an economic future as successful as their last few decades.

Surrounded by bales of material ready for reprocessing into new cloth, a Prato textile worker sorts a pile of rags into different colours and fibres. The used fabrics will be saturated with acid, then heated to destroy impurities without damaging the yarn.

THE BACK-STREET ENTREPRENEURS OF PRATO

Enjoying a per capita income 50 per cent higher than the national average, the workers of Prato, a town north-west of Florence, have every reason to believe that "small is beautiful". With a population of only 160,000 people, Prato boasts no fewer than 15,000 textile workshops, of which 13,000 have 10 or fewer employees—often members belonging to the same family.

The town's reputation as a centre of the rag trade was established in the 14th century by one Francesco di Marco Datini, who invented the bill of exchange and won lucrative markets in London, Bruges and Florence for the town's weavers of woollen cloth. In the same spirit of free enterprise, Prato's entrepreneurs restored the town's prosperity after World War II by recycling rags into clothing for Europe's millions of demobbed soldiers.

Since the 1970s, some of Prato's largest factories had to close because of foreign competition, but smaller family workshops, weaving every sort of yarn, have prospered. They owe their success partly to their low overheads, but mostly to their size, which enables them to react quickly to changes of fashion.

Women scrutinize rolls of material in a Prato factory which specializes in textile finishes—napping, for example, to raise velvety textures. Relatively large and sophisticated outfits such as this are in the minority, and they generally subcontract segments of their work to smaller family firms.

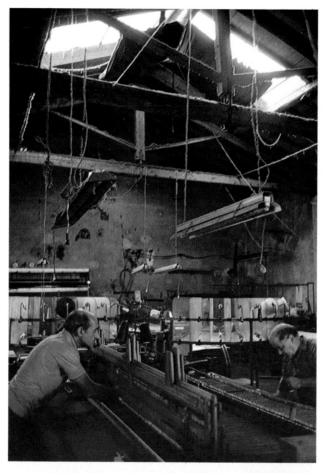

In a workshop in Prato's suburbs, two brothers operate a loom. Traditionally, small businesses were scattered throughout the town. Nowadays, however, with increased noise and pollution generated by the machines, the authorities are encouraging firms to move just outside the city.

While his two sons and dog remain absorbed in their own thoughts, a Prato weaver services a machine used in his husband-and-wife business. The casual air of such enterprises belies their profitability: the town's 1980 export earnings from textiles amounted to 1.5 billion dollars.

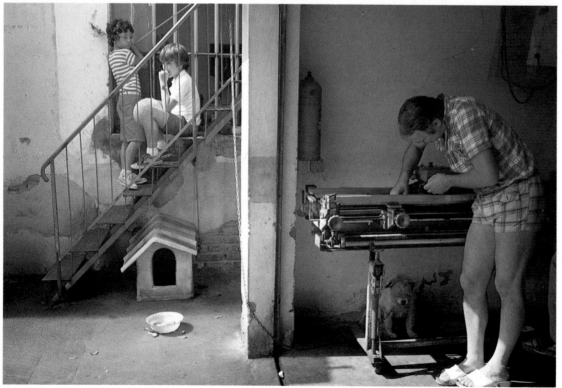

Living and working under the same roof, three generations crowd a workshop while their gun dogs compete for attention. Prato's self-employed cling to peasant traditions: they work long hours, but take time off to go shooting or to tend the vegetable plots that many keep near the town.

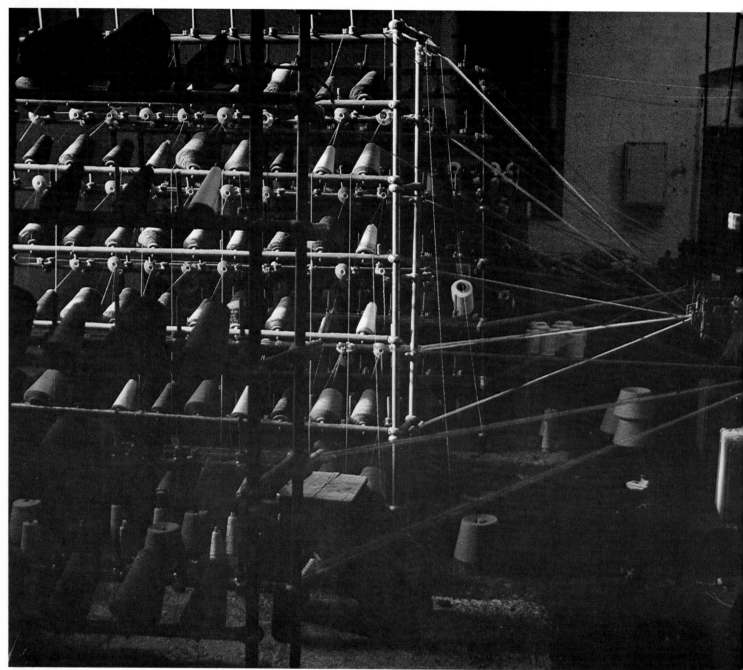

Coloured threads—destined to become the warp of a patterned fabric—converge on a machine operated by a 70-year-old woman.

A watchful dog keeps its mistress company as she winds white yarn on to a giant spool.

6

In Bologna, where local government has been in Communist hands since 1946, a nun attends a Party meeting. Pope Pius XII threatened Catholic Communists with excommunication in the 1940s, but today's relationship is one of *rapprochement*, stressing common concerns such as famine relief.

THE VOTERS' DILEMMA

To most outsiders, Italy seems to have the most unstable political system in Europe. Governments come and go with extraordinary regularity, and the average duration of post-war administrations has been just 11 months. For weeks at a stretch, Italians survive with a government in virtual suspension, while politicians from four or five parties strive to weld together the next short-lived coalition.

Yet appearances are misleading, because the parties that regularly take a share in government, and the pool of characters from which the senior ministers are drawn, have remained virtually the same for decades. Indeed, one could argue that Italy is politically the most stable country in Europe. The Christian Democrats, a party of the centre, emerged after World War II as the strongest grouping, and in the General Election of 1948, the first under Italy's new republican constitution, they were confirmed in power. Since then, they have dominated every one of more than 40 governments, first in alliance with other centre and some right-wing parties, later sometimes with the Socialists. The Communists, the other major party, have remained exiled in permanent opposition. Each time the ruling coalition collapses, the crisis is resolved by the creation of a new balance of power that is almost indistinguishable from the old.

The Constituent Assembly that hammered out the new republic's system of government in 1946 and 1947 did not reckon on the succession of government collapses that have convulsed the surface of Italian politics. The underlying stability was, however, something they consciously strove for. Their overriding aim was to prevent a tyrant like Mussolini rising to the top, so they diffused power as evenly as possible throughout the system.

Thus Italy has two parliamentary chambers with similar powers, except that only the Chamber of Deputies may initiate legislation. The other chamber, the Senate, has a few appointed members, but the vast majority of its delegates, and the whole of the Chamber of Deputies, are elected by the purest form of proportional representation. Unlike, say, West Germany or Norway, there is no minimum percentage of the nation's vote that a party must receive before it wins representation.

Parliament elects a president for a seven-year term. This figurehead wields even less authority than Italy's king did in the days of constitutional monarchy. The president cannot issue executive decrees; he can, after consultation with the parties, summon a political leader he thinks might be able to form a government with a majority in Parliament. In theory, the president can dissolve Parliament; in practice, he needs the parties' agreement.

The constitution accounts for many of the striking features of the Italian political scene, both good and bad. The weakness of the president, for example, contributes to the surface instability: unlike, say, France, with its strong presidency, Italy has nobody who can impose real sanctions and deadlines on bickering parliamentarians. The electoral system also contributes to Italy's succession of shortlived ministries by allowing many small parties a voice in Parliament—with the result that no large party ever commands an overall majority, and coalition government is inescapable. The government's programme is a laboriously negotiated compromise between the policies of the various parties; if promises are broken or legislation is delayed, a single party may withdraw from the coalition and wipe out its majority.

But the Italian electoral system also contributes to longer-term stability— amounting almost to paralysis—by ensuring that Parliament faithfully represents the voters' choice. One reason the pattern of parties has remained so constant is that small shifts in allegiance are not distorted into large alterations in parliamentary composition. There have been innumerable occasions since the war when the electorate seemed poised to make a definite break with the tradition of rule by the Christian Democrats and their smaller allies. But always, when the votes were counted, Italians were found to have returned to their traditional loyalties. Such change as did take place was gradual—so gradual, indeed, that the Italians have developed an obsession with decimals. If anyone was so ignorant as to venture that the Socialists polled 10 per cent of the vote in 1983, he would be corrected: "No, it was 10.7 per cent."

The slow pace of change may be because Italians take their politics very seriously. They affect an outer cynicism towards the political class in

6

DEVOLVING POLITICAL POWER

PRESIDENT

PRIME MINISTER

CABINET

CHAMBER OF DEPUTIES

SENATE

NATIONAL   PARLIAMENT

PREFECTS

CONTROL COMMISSIONS

PROVINCIAL COUNCILS

REGIONAL COUNCILS

COMMUNAL COUNCILS

MAYORS

ELECTORATE

DIRECT ELECTION   INDIRECT ELECTION   APPOINTMENT   SUPERVISORY POWERS

Italy is a republic with a parliamentary system of government, designed to restrict the powers vested in any individual. The head of state is the president, elected for a seven-year term by Parliament, who is not involved in the day-to-day running of the country. The executive consists of the prime minister, appointed by the president, and a Cabinet, selected by the prime minister.

Parliament is composed of two houses of equal status, which duplicate each other's activities—the Chamber of Deputies, with elected members, and the Senate. While most of the 315 senators are elected, a handful are life appointments of the president. Parliament handles a large number of private members' bills, but the bulk of its work is the processing of legislation originated by the government.

Besides voting for national representatives, Italians also elect three tiers of local deputies. The smallest units of local government are the 8,086 communes, each run by elected councillors and a mayor. Limited local revenues restrict the councillors' scope, and at any breakdown of their functions, the prefect—a civil servant appointed by the president on the advice of the Cabinet—can assume control.

At the next level of local government are 95 provinces, also administered by elected councils. On a still higher plane, the elected representatives of the 20 regions have wide powers of legislative action over such fields as local planning and health services, but their measures must be ratified by a centrally appointed Control Commission.

general—"they're all crooks" is a common refrain. But the floating, rather flippant vote in the centre of the American and British political spectrum is almost unknown in Italy: voting habits are the product of class, region, religion, family and intellectual evolution in a way that would surprise people in most Western democracies. Turnout is invariably high: at general elections, it rarely falls below 80 per cent, and in regional and local elections 70 to 80 per cent turnouts are common. These figures are boosted by the fact that voting is deemed a civic duty in Italy, and failure to vote can be noted on police records; an applicant for a civil service post who has omitted to vote may have some explaining to do. Nonetheless, the figures are impressive.

The responsible, cautious attitude of voters has been reinforced by the more than usually difficult choice they face. With the Communists as the main opposition party, any abandonment of the status quo would be a leap in the dark that the majority of Italian voters have been unwilling to contemplate. In the early post-war years, a vote for the Communist Party appeared to many to mean a vote to join the Soviet bloc. The Italian Communist Party has increasingly distanced itself from Moscow, but a residue of fear has remained; whenever the Communists have looked in danger of significantly increasing their share of the poll, the Christian Democrats have been able to cry wolf, scaring wavering constituents back into their time-tested allegiances.

France, like Italy, found itself with a large, well-organized Communist Party after the war; the majority of its electorate, like the Italians, rejected the option it represented and voted for years for right-of-centre governments.

The tiered seats and balconies of the Chamber of Deputies in Rome—one of the two Italian houses of Parliament—provide a theatrical setting for Italy's lawmakers. Above the parliamentarians is a frieze which illustrates the rise of Italian civilization.

6

But in France, the Socialist Party was able to reconstruct itself during the late 1960s and overtake the Communists as a major party of the left, making a left-wing government acceptable by 1981. The Italian Socialists have never attained that position and only since the late 1970s have they become a force to be reckoned with in politics. For most of the post-war period, Italians have been denied any realistic left-wing option other than the Communists.

Perhaps the best place to see the paradoxical steadiness of Italian politics is in a small town. It is there, away from the crowds and banner-waving demonstrators of Rome or Turin or Milan, that Italian democracy finds its indispensable bedrock.

Like so many other aspects of small-town life, politics finds its expression, though peaceably enough, out in the streets. It does not dominate: on market days or any other time when people gather, the loudest arguments are likely to be about football teams. But somewhere or another there are bound to be a few party political journals pinned up on public display. The Communist *Unitá* (Unity) will certainly be one of them; so, most likely, will be the Socialist *Avanti!* (Forward) and the Christian Democrat *Il Popolo.* Around each will be a little knot of the *pro* and the *contro*, quietly discussing the issues of the day.

More interesting than the party press are the party posters with which each faction conducts its interminable warfare with the others. These are not the kind of poster that every party's Rome headquarters churns out for national distribution at election time, but the hand-printed—and often hand-written—broadsheets by which local squabbles are given a good, ill-tempered airing. The parties always retain their national character: it can be disconcerting to see the panoply of Marxist jargon deployed in the service of a feud about too many municipal contracts going to the wrong brother-in-law. And only in Italy would a Communist mayor who is also a prosperous businessman denounce his rivals for "anti-proletarianism". Such campaigns rarely incite riots, but at least the population knows what is going on.

When national elections come round, the professional politicians take a hand. The arrival of such a man for an election meeting in a small Italian town presents a rare study in contrasts. On the platform, guarded by tough-looking *carabinieri* and backed by even tougher-looking party henchmen, he will launch into his set speech. Probably, it will be as full of platitudes as such orations usually are in other countries. But it will be delivered with a peculiarly Italian intensity and in high rhetorical style, illustrated with the gestures of a 19th-century tragedian. The audience will listen in a polite silence that is equally studied, interrupting occasionally with a ripple of applause. Then they will quietly leave.

Election day itself is just as low-key. It will be a Sunday, the most social day of the Italian week, and it will be more than usually social because many friends and relations, now living far from home, have taken advantage of the free rail tickets provided by the government to encourage them to return to their native *comune* to vote.

Throughout the day, in a sort of attenuated *passeggiata*, people will amble to and from the polling station. That temple of democracy will be guarded by a teenage conscript soldier, armed with nothing more ferocious than a scabbarded dress bayonet and—if it is hot and no superior is nearby—an ice-cream cone. Around the polling station there will be much banter between political opponents but rarely bitter abuse. If the party a man supports goes on to win a few more percentage points of the poll, he will not expect the millennium to arrive tomorrow. If his party is knocked back a little, he will not anticipate the end of the world.

Ordinary Italians, loyal though they may be to their party, are all too aware of the gap between politicians' manifestos and their actions. No matter how sincere the election promises, each party is hobbled by its coalition partners. Only if it can bring other parties round to its way of thinking can it effect change. For this reason, the stuff of Italian politics is power bargaining rather than policy statements, alliances rather than issues.

The Christian Democrats, the party that kept back the left-wing tide for so long, are masters of the art of political survival. They trace their ancestry to the Italian Popular Party, founded in 1919 by the priest Don Luigi Sturzo. Forced underground by Mussolini and the Pope, they emerged during the Cold War of the late 1940s as a coalition of anti-Communist forces.

The party has drawn on four main power bases. The first, the Church, was especially important in the early post-war years but has declined in significance as the priests' hold on Italians has diminished. In its Catholic schools and universities, the Church once trained much of the senior leadership of the party; it also provided a natural hustings—the pulpit.

The second reservoir of support has been the south, together with most of

In the Sala Clementina, vestibule of the papal apartments, Italian bishops await an audience with the Pope. By Church law, all Catholic bishops must travel to the Vatican every 10 years and report to the Pontiff on diocesan affairs.

Italy's mountain regions. Old people predominate in these areas—the young have left for the cities of the industrial north—and it is among the old that fear of Communism has been greatest. In the early post-war years, the Christian Democrats undertook extensive land reforms in the poorer rural regions, appropriating farms from the big landlords and parcelling them out to the peasants. These landowners became ultra-conservative and unshakable supporters of the party. But the main reason for its continuing strength is unashamed vote-buying; jobs throughout the sprawling bureaucracy are available only to party loyalists. Self-seeking officialdom has been a feature of southern life for centuries, and the Christian Democrats have efficiently harnessed the tradition for their own ends.

The third power base of the Christian Democrats has been the middle class, which, however, has increasingly strayed to vote for smaller parties. Yet even when bourgeois support was at its strongest, Christian Democrats prided themselves in representing the whole class spectrum, rather than just the comfortably placed; indeed, their fourth power base has been a Catholic trade union wing.

With such diverse support, the Christian Democrats have avoided being pinned too precisely to any given point on the left-right spectrum. They could not be described as a typical Western European Conservative party, since they have not placed especial stress on private enterprise and are in favour of a large state-owned industrial sector. They have been fairly responsive to social change within Italy; they have initiated low-cost housing in the major cities, created a health service, and enacted a number of laws protecting employees from exploitation. But they are not altogether a welfare state party either, because they believe that members of families must be helped to look after each other, rather than relying on the state to take over; thus, they expect working people to take in their ageing parents rather than look to the state to provide homes.

The man who forged the modern Christian Democrat Party and who

6

formulated its philosophy was Alcide de Gasperi, a devout Catholic who led a succession of governments from 1946 to 1953. He was an impressive, statesmanlike figure, but his firm leadership eventually ran aground on the political rivalries between different factions of his party. Factionalism has riddled the party ever since. There are always four or five "currents" with slightly different aims and emphases, which battle continuously for dominance. One result is that each new government generally has a different prime minister from the previous one, the fresh face at the top representing a different clique within the party which has temporarily gained ascendancy.

After the de Gasperi era, the party was dominated by a personal rivalry between two men, Amintore Fanfani and Aldo Moro. Two more opposite figures could hardly be imagined: Fanfani was small, irrepressible, brilliantly articulate, as aggressive as a bull terrier, constantly urging the party in new directions. In the early 1960s, he was the architect of a *rapprochement* with the Socialists. Moro was a tall, gangly, awkward intellectual, given to arcane political manoeuvring and interminable, rambling speeches (he coined the much-mocked phrase "parallel convergences"). His principal goal appeared to be a reconciliation between the Christian Democrats and the Communist Party. Moro's delicate negotiations with the Communists were cut short in 1978 when he was assassinated by terrorists. He was replaced as leader of the left wing of his party by Giulio Andreotti, a stooped figure with a sardonic wit and priestly demeanour who became the party's ablest intriguer.

The seesawing fortunes of the factions within the party cannot mask an overall decline in its fortunes. In the 1948 elections it took nearly half the nation's vote; in the 1980s, it attracted only one third. Its main difficulty is simply its long hold on power, not just in national but also in local and regional government, which has made it a home for ambitious place seekers. Over the years it has been blemished by a succession of scandals.

In the mid-1970s, prominent Christian Democrats were implicated in the Lockheed affair, in which senior officials of the Ministry of Defence were alleged to have taken bribes from executives of the Lockheed company to buy their aircraft. The charges even touched the circle surrounding the nation's President, Giovanni Leone—another Christian Democrat—who was forced to resign in 1978. The scandal of the early 1980s centred on the activities of Freemasons, especially in a lodge codenamed P2. There were allegations that the group served as a "state within a state" and had connections with the Mafia and other underworld figures. Lists found by magistrates included not only judges, army officers and members of the security services, but also many eminent Christian Democrats.

The Christian Democrats are also associated with Italy's administrative paralysis. Patronage is so integral to the bureaucracy that far-reaching social reform is impossible under the party's aegis. Any major spending initiative—the Government's Fund for the South, for example, or the reform of the health service, or even emergency relief for earthquake victims—has become a pot of gold to be divided up among local government officials. Such problems should not be exaggerated: they are common to political parties in most countries that have undergone rapid industrialization, and Italy has made astonishing strides despite them. But the mud clings to the party's name.

The Communists, by contrast, cultivate an image of irreproachable purity. This claim is largely borne out by their record in municipal government; since 1975, they have run most of Italy's big cities in alliance with the Socialists, and on the whole they have kept their hands clean. But of as much interest to the average Italian is their claim to be totally committed to democracy. Over several decades, they have undergone a soul-searching evolution from an orthodox replica of the Soviet mould into what looks remarkably like a Western-style socialist party.

The germ of the Italian Communist heresy was sown in the 1920s and 1930s by Antonio Gramsci, the party's founder. He was an intellectual who spent years in Fascist jails. There he evolved the theory that the Communist Party should substitute the goal of the "hegemony of the proletariat" for the classic Marxist doctrine of the "dictatorship of the proletariat". Hairsplitting though it may seem at first sight, the implication of Gramsci's formula was vast: the middle classes would not be totally deprived of any say in government, but would no longer be allowed to dominate the workers.

Nonetheless, in the early post-war years there was not much to choose between the Italian Communist Party and those of Eastern Europe. Stalinists were prominent among its members. Most of its funds came either as grants from the Soviet Union or from a party-controlled import-export agency which licensed deals with the countries of the Eastern bloc. Much of the party's support came from disaffected landless

A MINIATURE STATE WITHIN A STATE

In the heart of Rome, a yellow and white flag declares the sovereignty of 44 walled hectares of palaces, gardens, museums and churches. It is the flag of Vatican City, temporal domain of the Pope. This territory houses a shifting population of around a thousand and provides a politically independent base for the Pope's larger sphere—the Holy See, which governs the faith of Catholics.

With diplomatic ties to nearly 100 countries, the Holy See is an international power influencing any trouble spot where its faithful are in number. Its civil service, the Curia, administers farflung pastoral and evangelical work, as well as handling the complex and secret Vatican finances. Although Vatican City is only a remnant of the once sprawling Papal States, the Pope's spiritual jurisdiction continues to grow as the worldwide Catholic population approaches 800 million.

1. **St. Peter's Basilica—the world's largest church, built above the tomb reputed to hold St. Peter's remains.**
2. **The Apostolic Palace, which accommodates the papal apartments and leading departments of the Curia.**
3. **The Government Palace—central offices for the administration of the city-state and its art collection.**
4. **The Audience Hall—an auditorium built in 1971 to seat up to 7,000 at weekly audiences with the Pope.**
5. **The Vatican Library—a collection of some one million books and documents.**
6. **Vatican Radio—a station broadcasting throughout the world, with religious programmes and news in 32 languages.**
7. **Offices of *Osservatore Romano*, the Vatican newspaper with a circulation of 50,000, which publishes church news and complete texts of papal speeches.**
8. **The Polyglot Press, publisher of missionary texts and papal encyclicals.**
9. **The Swiss Guards' Barracks—home of the Vatican Security Force, 100 Catholic soldiers from Switzerland.**
10. **The Sistine Chapel—meeting-place of Cardinals, who elect new Popes beneath a ceiling by Michelangelo.**

peasants on large estates in what has come to be known as Italy's "red belt"—the regions of Tuscany, Emilia-Romagna and Umbria. There were also votes from the masses streaming from the countryside to the cities, with their abysmal social services and housing. Both constituencies wanted drastic changes in Italian society.

By the early 1970s, the Communists were also winning a following among intellectuals who were disillusioned with Christian Democratic rule. This development placed the party's leadership in a dilemma. To continue winning adherents among the middle classes, the Communists realized they had to distance themselves further from the Soviet model, which was tarnished as a result of the invasions of Hungary in 1956 and Czechoslovakia in 1968. The Italian working class, benefiting from consumer goods for the first time, also began to have its doubts about the virtues of a society in which there would be no private property.

The great leap forward to democratic acceptability came in 1976, after a general election in which the Communist vote shot from 27 to 34 per cent. At this time, the head of the Communist Party was Enrico Berlinguer, the small, dour scion of a minor Sardinian aristocratic family. The liberal wing of the party secured an unequivocal statement from Berlinguer that the leadership was committed to democracy, indeed that it valued democracy above socialism; it accepted the ballot box as the only route to power. The party even began to make its first, timid criticisms of the Soviet model. It stressed the need for economic planning and for more social spending in Italy, but had no plans to nationalize more of the economy than was already in public hands. It

Children play in the grounds of their kindergarten, converted from a church. Some 75 per cent of Bolognese children attend city nurseries.

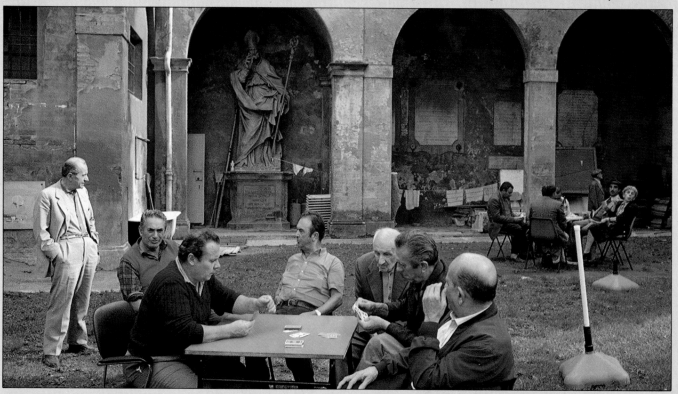

Senior citizens play cards in the garden of a municipal community centre, a facility which also mounts exhibitions and plays.

SHOWPIECE OF ITALIAN COMMUNISM

Bologna's characteristic arcades line a quiet street.

The university town of Bologna is a procession of arcades, whose red stone porticoes flank nearly every street and square. Behind the medieval colonnades, however, contemporary political dramas are played out, for Bologna is a Communist municipality, the only sizeable Italian city to be governed by a predominantly Communist majority continuously since the end of World War II.

With a city council that has often been held up as the most efficient and least corrupt in Italy, Bologna is a shop window for Communist achievements on a local scale. Its most radical reform has been the decentralization of city government. In a system unique for Italy, Bologna is divided into 18 wards, each with its own council mediating between the mayor and the people. The city has tackled urban problems, with successful programmes of traffic reform, nursery education and health care for the elderly.

The city council's most ambitious project has been in housing. With their magnificent but dilapidated architectural heritage threatened by bulldozing developers after World War II, the Communists became conservationists. Their plan, still under way, has rescued the historic district by adapting it to modern needs. Old palaces now house public libraries and community centres, dubbed Houses of the People; an old convent is home to a nursery school.

In the historic city centre, with some 70,000 residents, the municipality buys properties at low prices and temporarily rehouses their occupants. After each dwelling is structurally repaired and fitted with plumbing, electricity and central heating, the original owners return. Larger buildings, such as churches and palaces, are restored before appropriate civic functions are found for them. Bending the Marxist line with typically Italian ease, the Bolognese Communists have co-opted local capitalists to fund part of the conservation scheme.

accepted, in principle, that Italy should remain a member of NATO.

In the years that followed, the party resisted a formal break with the Soviet Union, and kept up its habit of bitterly criticizing everything about the United States: its society, its capitalist ethic and, especially, its foreign policy. It refused to eject its remaining handful of Stalinists, as its critics demanded. But despite the Italian Communists' lingering fondness for the Soviet Union, it seemed clear by the time of Berlinguer's sudden death in 1984 that they were committed to a separate path.

Berlinguer did much to quell fears of Communist power, but he failed to bring his party into government. In 1976, it looked as though there was a chance of the Communists entering the cabinet. The Socialists, who had been in a series of coalitions with the Christian Democrats, refused to join another government, so the ruling party was compelled to seek support elsewhere. Insisting that the Communists lacked the democratic credentials to join the government, the party's leaders refused to offer them ministerial places, but did agree to consult them on major issues in return for support in Parliament and outside. Berlinguer accepted this nebulous arrangement because it seemed a foot in the door of power and a step towards his dream of a "historic compromise" coalition with the Christian Democrats and Socialists. But after the assassination of Aldo Moro in 1978, Berlinguer found, to his surprise, that the Christian Democrats were refusing to move any closer. A year later, in frustration, he withdrew his support and the government fell.

Failure to achieve the historic compromise forced Berlinguer to look for an alternative strategy. Alliance with

149

6

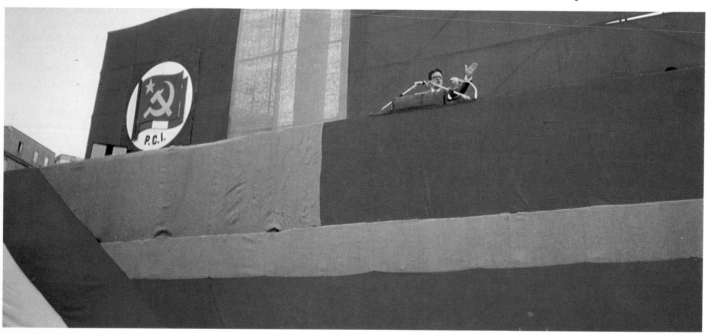

the non-Communist left became the Communist Party's official policy, although a large part of the Berlinguer wing of the party still hankered after a deal with the Christian Democrats.

The Socialist Party could have been the main alternative to the Christian Democrats, were it not for two near mortal blows that crippled the party in the 1940s and 1960s respectively. The first was an alliance with the Communists in 1948, which chased many moderate politicians out of the party and scared away many voters. The later blow was the long association with the Christian Democrats from 1963, which led many voters to view the Socialists as the Christian Democrats' poodle.

Shaky strategy was not the least of the Socialists' problems; they also suffered a perpetual identity crisis. In the early post-war years, they regarded the Communists, rather suspiciously, as brothers, but differentiated themselves by stressing their own allegiance to democracy and the Western alliance. When, in the 1970s, the Communists announced that they, too, were in favour of democracy and NATO, the Socialists were left without distinguishing traits. It was not until the end of the decade that they found a fresh role, thanks to a new leader, Bettino Craxi.

Craxi, a tall, thickset man with a stubborn, pug-like expression and a lightning intellect, took over as Secretary in 1976. Within months, he was imposing his stamp on the party. He replaced its symbol—the hammer and sickle, which had represented the party's links with the workers—with a carnation. He denounced the Communist Party—even in its reformist, post-Berlinguer mode—as "Stalinist". He insisted that the welfare state should be streamlined, and espoused pro-environmental policies. And then, having reshaped the party, Craxi turned his attention to making the Socialists once more a force in politics.

After the 1979 election, when the Christian Democratic–Communist alliance broke up amid mutual recriminations, Craxi made it clear that he would co-operate with the Christian Democrats, but only for a high price: nothing less than the direction of government policy and the post of prime minister. Initially, he had to make do with a compromise candidate—the leader of the small, left-of-centre Republican Party, Giovanni Spadolini, who in 1981 became the first non-Christian Democratic prime minister since 1945. But by 1983 he was granted the position he had so long coveted.

Craxi acted decisively from the first days of his administration. The government soon raised Italy's international profile and took a tough anti-Soviet line; it was, for example, far more enthusiastic than previous administrations about the siting of NATO anti-Soviet missiles on Italian soil. On the domestic front, Craxi dared to tackle the wage indexation which had been sacrosanct since 1975, and succeeded in partly cutting the link between inflation and automatic wage rises.

In 1984, he exchanged conciliatory notes with the Communist Party, which had been wooing the Socialists since the start of the 1980s but had received no friendly response. The move brilliantly exploited the Socialists' pivotal position. Despite his party's meagre share of the votes, Craxi had compelled the majority party to depend on him, while for the first time holding out the real possibility of a left-wing alliance that would put the Christian Democrats in opposition.

Italy's colourful smaller parties between them attract some 20 per cent of the vote at general elections. These parties perform several vital functions, notably to serve as lightning conductors for those who are disaffected with the Christian Democrats but who do not want to vote for the left, and to act as independent checks on incompetence and corruption in government.

The biggest of the minor parties, the far-right Italian Social Movement, has become the pariah of Italian politics. The party is vigorously nationalist and fiercely anti-Christian Democratic. The inspiration of Mussolini's regime is evident, though the Italian Social Movement denies being a fascist party; if it admitted to the label, it would be banned by Italian law. It draws its support from the lower middle class, from

nostalgics with fond memories of Il Duce, and from young people who yearn for novelty and adventure.

Some politicians in the party have been accused of connections with terrorism and plots against the state. The leadership has striven to distance itself from these extremists. Their efforts have met with only partial success. Opponents continue to charge the party with anti-democratic aspirations, and under no foreseeable circumstances would the Christian Democrats ask it to join a right-of-centre coalition.

To the immediate right of the Christian Democrats is the Liberal Party, representing the interests of the land-owning class and of the very hautest *haute bourgeoisie*. The Liberals are persuasive advocates of monetarist economics and of the Western alliance; the Christian Democrats consider them acceptable coalition partners.

The Social Democrats began as an anti-Communist party that broke away from the Socialists in the 1940s, but have softened their traditional hostility to the Communists a little in recent years. A large part of their support comes from their stalwart defence of Italy's pension system, which acts as a covert government subsidy for millions of Italians for whom it was never intended (some five million Italians draw disability pensions, for example, and most of them are able-bodied). Party members have been implicated in a number of scandals, including the P2 masonic lodge affair, when the party's leader, Pietro Longo, resigned as budget minister in 1984, but the Social Democrats remain a staple of every government coalition.

The Republican Party is the conscience and brain of Italian politics. With only about one Italian in 20 vot-

ing for it, its influence far outweighs its size. Under Ugo La Malfa, a politician of immense stature, it established itself as the party calling for sound finance, a functioning welfare state, and honesty in public life. La Malfa was succeeded by Giovanni Spadolini, a roly-poly former editor of Italy's main newspaper, *Corriere della Sera*. His nomination as prime minister in 1981 was a measure of the party's status. Spadolini's government achieved little, but the high moral tone of its public utterances impressed many Italians.

The Radicals started as a pressure group outside Parliament; in the early 1970s, they campaigned successfully against repealing the new divorce law, and in favour of abortion law reform. By 1976, their first delegates were returned to the Chamber of Deputies. Under the stentorian leadership of Marco Pannella, the party adopted minority causes such as homosexual rights. They also took a strong pro-ecology stand. They reached their peak of popularity in the late 1970s; in subsequent years, voters grew weary of their constant internal bickering and especially of Pannella's strident appetite for self-publicity, which on one occasion led him to exchange blows with several Communists on the floor of the Chamber of Deputies.

Among the other parties represented in Parliament are generally one or more from the far left—splinters from the Communist Party which advocate the revolutionary overthrow of the system. Their numbers are too small to make much impact.

Italy still has minorities on both extremes which oppose the parliamentary system altogether. The far right's strategy, such as it is, is to inflame

6

emotions by acts of violence so that gang warfare breaks out; in the ensuing panic, they think that an authoritarian government would be welcomed. Neo-Fascists were almost certainly responsible for a number of bomb attacks, including an assault on a Milan bank in 1969 and a large explosion at Brescia. The most horrifying incident was a bombing at Bologna railway station in 1980, which took more than 80 lives.

But the number of those involved in right-wing terrorism has never been large, and the threat from the far right has faded in recent years. The armed forces have never shown the same interest in politics as those of other Latin countries, and without their support the extreme right is unlikely to make much headway politically.

If the far right has shown itself to be sporadically murderous but a political failure, the same cannot be said of the far left, which held Italian democracy at bay for four years from 1976 to 1980. The origins of left-wing terrorism can be traced back to the student and labour unrest of 1968–1969, when a wave of demonstrations ruffled the inertia of Italian politics. Many of the protestors believed that there was no dislodging the Christian Democrats through parliamentary means, and that the Communists were too restrained in their tactics. Changes in the university system, which virtually guaranteed anyone a place at college, irrespective of the limited teaching facilities and the even more limited job opportunities for humanities graduates, fuelled the frustrations of young people.

There developed a loose extra-parliamentary grouping of those who opposed the system altogether. It was called Autonomy, and it may have had as many as 150,000 adherents at its peak in the early 1970s. Autonomy's leaders were radical university professors, and its intellectual base was in Padua. Within Autonomy, a more organized movement coalesced, from whose ranks were drawn the three main terrorist groups of the decade—the Red Brigades, whose recruits came largely from middle-class backgrounds, the working-class Armed Proletarian Nuclei, which operated in Naples and the south, and Front Line, a looser and more disparate organization than the other two. Myriad smaller groups also sprang up.

The founders of the Red Brigades were a married couple, Margherita ("Mara") Cagol and Renato Curcio, who had been sociology students together at the University of Trento. Comfortably off, apparently destined for careers in chemistry and accounting respectively, they instead drifted underground and began to see themselves as the élite leadership that would bring about the revolution on behalf of the masses. By the early 1970s, they had built up a clandestine military organization around them. Its objective was to set up an "armed party" that would overthrow the diseased organs of the Italian state, or would provoke such a counter-reaction from the authorities that the proletarians would flock to join their ranks. There was much speculation about possible international connections between the Red Brigades and Czechoslovakia, the Palestinians or Libya, among others, but none received definite confirmation.

In the early days, the Red Brigades' crimes consisted mainly of damage to property—burning the cars of factory bosses, for example—but, becoming bolder and more vicious, they graduated to armed robbery and murder.

From shooting policemen, the Brigades progressed to shooting journalists, magistrates (in an effort to prevent their comrades being tried), industrialists and, eventually, politicians.

By 1978, Mara Cagol was dead, mown down in a shoot-out with the police, and Renato Curcio had been tracked down and imprisoned. He and a number of other founders were awaiting their trial, which was repeatedly put off for fear of reprisals. Only momentarily nonplussed by the disappearance of their leaders, the Red Brigades had rallied themselves and quickly evolved into a more deadly and efficient organ than ever before.

Their forces were now elaborately subdivided into almost autonomous cells, ensuring near-perfect security for the upper ranks and for each independent branch no matter how many of the humble operatives were captured. All ranks, however, submitted themselves to the rigid, almost monastic rules prescribed for daily life. Hair was to be cut short, beards were forbidden, meals were to be eaten at home, bedtime was before midnight, apartments were to be kept clean and tidy, guns were to be carried at all times.

With this discipline, the Red Brigades were capable of carrying out more elaborate crimes than ever before. Meticulously, they developed plans to stage a master-coup. Their goal was nothing less than to capture Italy's leading politician.

On the morning of March 16, ex-prime minister Aldo Moro was being driven to Parliament from the small church he attended daily. Followed by an escort vehicle, his car moved slowly down Rome's Via Fani. A car suddenly backed into the street, blocking the way forward. Moro's chauffeur jammed on the brakes and the escort crashed into the back of the car.

The ambushers jumped from their car and sprayed the scene with bullets. Moro was seized and manhandled into a waiting vehicle. The kidnappers then sped off, leaving the corpses of the bodyguards lying in the street.

Moro was held for nearly two months by his Red Brigade captors. While the police searched fruitlessly, pictures of him in his captivity were circulated, together with letters which he was somehow induced or forced to write, pleading for negotiations to be opened and hinting at dark revelations he might be obliged to make. Then on May 9, after a tipoff, police discovered his body in the boot of a Renault, parked as a symbolic gesture half-way between the Christian Democratic and Communist headquarters in central Rome. It was a supreme gesture of contempt for authority by the terrorists.

But the coldblooded murder won no sympathy among the public; and the state reacted to it with commendable restraint, by introducing laws of pre-ventive detention (since withdrawn) that only marginally tightened existing legislation. The tide began to turn against the terrorists.

At this crucial point, a new interior minister, Virginio Rognoni, was appointed to oversee Italy's three main police forces—the *carabinieri* or armed police, the treasury police, whose original role of tracking down tax evaders has expanded in many directions, and the regular police. Carlo Alberto Dalla Chiesa, a *carabiniere* general, was appointed head of an élite anti-terrorist detachment. To break the shield of secrecy with which the Brigades protected themselves, a law was passed allowing terrorists who informed on their comrades to receive considerably reduced prison sentences.

Aided by this measure, Dalla Chiesa scored spectacular successes in cracking Red Brigades' cells. His technique was to insert one man into a cell or "column" which was in contact with another cell only through a single member. The infiltrator would identify who the key member was; the police would then arrest and interrogate him, using the prospect of the reduced jail sentence as an inducement for him to talk. The Milan column of the Red Brigades was the first to be thoroughly broken; the Genoa, Turin and Rome columns followed shortly afterwards. Some 400 arrests of suspected terrorists were made in less than three years. By 1982, terrorism had been all but defeated in Italy, the Red Brigades themselves acknowledging that their dream of a civil war in Italy was lost.

Dalla Chiesa's success in dealing with the Red Brigades was so spectacular that the government of the day decided to employ him in tackling more deep-rooted problems: the Mafia, its Calabrian cousin the 'Ndrangheta and the Neapolitan Camorra. But the outcome was very different. Just four months after Dalla Chiesa had been sent to Palermo, he was shot dead in the city centre by Mafia gunmen.

This catastrophe did not deter the Italian government from continuing the battle against the Mafia. In the mid-1980s, notable progress was made in rounding up Mafia criminals, once again by encouraging key figures to talk. But even the most optimistic of Italians are resigned to a long, hard

Political slogans are outnumbered by declarations of love among the graffiti splashed across a Roman bridge. The messages are a modern manifestation of an old Italian impulse: the walls of Pompeii carry political and amorous scribblings from the first century A.D.

6

struggle against the Mafia and the other secret organizations before they can be overcome.

The Italian state's successful fight against terrorism showed it at its decisive best. But in less grave situations, firm leadership is all too rare. The system militates against it. Because of faction-fighting within the parties and the danger of the strongest party alienating any one of its coalition partners, all change must be reached by consensus, a slow and painful business. One result is that governments invariably have great difficulty in enforcing their authority on other institutions—on trade unions, employers and the bureaucracy, for example. The shortcomings of the system are also visible in the international field. The merry-go-round of Italian prime ministers has made it difficult for any one of them to acquire an international reputation. As a result, Italy has been less effective than the other major partners within NATO or the EEC in terms of making its voice heard, although its commitment to both is passionate.

Italians are well aware of the lack of decisive leadership, and proposals to remedy it abound. The Socialists, in particular, have pressed for constitutional reform. One possibility would be to strengthen the president's powers—but this is unlikely to find favour, as Italians recoil from any weakening of parliament. Another possibility is to strengthen the power of the prime minister vis-à-vis his own party and those in coalition with him. At present, though the premier has the right to choose his cabinet, he is in practice obliged to listen to the party secretaries—whose chief concern is that each faction gets its due share of seats.

Change in the electoral system has also been mooted, to allow only parties with 5 per cent or more of the vote to sit in Parliament; this would force the small parties to merge into bigger groups and might lead to more stable coalitions. But the very inertia of the political system makes radical constitutional reform unlikely in the near future.

Italians are fond of saying that they are governed best when they are not governed at all. That is untrue: Italy could be governed much more effectively than it is. However, the system is considerably more resilient than most outsiders realize, and Italians are more content with it than their grumbles suggest. The recurring government crises are so predictable that they do not unduly hold up the administrative processes and, despite the obstacles, surprisingly far-reaching reforms have been enacted.

Most fundamental and impressive is the fact that Italy has come through its post-war industrial revolution without succumbing to authoritarian rule. Few countries have experienced the development of an urban, manufacturing economy without suffering serious upheaval or repression. In Italy's Mediterranean neighbours, Greece and Turkey, political disturbances were followed by a bout of autocratic government; Spain and Portugal were ruled by dictators throughout the process of industrialization. Yet Italy managed to contain the social unrest engendered by its great drive towards national prosperity. For its stability, Italy must spare some gratitude for the constitution which guards against extremist tendencies. But most of all it must thank its level-headed voters, staunchly committed to their ramshackle, but functioning, democracy.

With swords frozen in salute, a detachment of the élite police corps, known as the Corazzieri, guards a corridor in the Quirinal Palace, the official presidential residence. Recruits for the unit—honour escort to the president and visiting heads of state—must be at least 1.90 metres tall.

ACKNOWLEDGEMENTS

The index for this book was prepared by Vicki Robinson. For their help with this volume the editors also wish to thank the following: Federica Bellici, Paolo Ricci, Italian Tourist Office, London; Mike Brown, London; Marco Cagnoni, Pietrasanta; Caposio e Lauria, Architects' Studio, Turin; Catholic Media Society, London; Windsor Chorlton, London; Conte Piero Milano d'Aragona, Turin; Conte Xavier de Maistre, Turin; Fiat Press Office, Turin; Caroline Hill, London; Martin Leighton, Hove; Jacqueline Long, The Lighting Workshop, London; Catherine Mcnabb, London; Simon Mitchell, Marcatré Limited, London; *La Nazione*, Prato, Enrico Nori, Carrara; Diego Novelli, Turin; Robin Olson, London; Vittorio Prayer, Town Council, Carrara; Enzo Ragazzini, Rome; Malise Ruthven, London; Renzo Salvadori, Venice; Roger Stewart, Sutton; Ruth Sullivan, London; Deborah Thompson, London; Unione Industriale, Prato; the staff of the Library of the Italian Institute, London.

PICTURE CREDITS

Credits from left to right are separated by semicolons, from top to bottom by dashes.

Cover: Dave Peterson from The Image Bank, London. Front endpaper: Map by Roger Stewart, London. Back endpaper: Digitized image by Creative Data, London.

1, 2: © Flag Research Center, Winchester, Massachusetts. **6, 7**: Romano Cagnoni, London. **8**: Digitized image by Creative Data, London. **8, 9**: Gerd Ludwig from Visum, Hamburg. **10, 11**: Romano Cagnoni, London. **12**: Digitized image by Creative Data, London. **12, 13**: Hans Wiesenhofer, Pöllau, Austria. **14, 15**: John G. Ross, Rome. **16**: Thomas Höpker from Bildagentur Anne Hamann, Munich. **18**: Romano Cagnoni, London. **19**: Thomas Höpker from Bildagentur Anne Hamann, Munich. **20**: Romano Cagnoni, London (2)—Hans Wiesenhofer, Pöllau, Austria. **21**: Steve Lipson, California—Helmut Gritscher from Aspect Picture Library, London—Gerd Ludwig from Visum, Hamburg. **23**: Gary Gladstone from The Image Bank, London. **25**: Francesco Paolo Cito, Naples. **26**: Carlo Chinca, London—Romano Cagnoni, London (2); Romano Cagnoni, London—Jonathan Blair from Black Star/Colorific!, London—Hans-Jürgen Burkard, Hamburg. **28**: Romano Cagnoni, London. **29**: Painting by Peter Jarvis of the Heraldry Society, London, adapted by Oxford Illustrators Ltd. **31**: Romano Cagnoni, London—Adam Woolfitt from Susan Griggs Agency, London. **32–39**: Romano Cagnoni, London. **40**: Aldo Durazzi, Rome. **42**: Romano Cagnoni, London. **43**: Courtesy of Palace of Conservators, Rome, photograph by

Erich Lessing from Magnum, Paris. **45**: Courtesy of Palazzo Vecchio, Florence, photograph by Scala, Florence. **46**: Head from statue of Apollo, courtesy of Museo Nazionale Etrusco di Villa Giulia, Rome, photograph by Mauro Pucciarelli, Rome; Kunsthistorisches Museum, Vienna—Erich Lessing from Magnum, Paris. **47**: Detail of stained glass window, photograph by Sonia Halliday and Laura Lushington, Weston Turville, England; courtesy of Sansovino Library, Venice, photograph by Adam Woolfitt from Susan Griggs Picture Agency, London; courtesy of the Bargello, photograph by Scala, Florence. **48**: Courtesy of the Istituto e Museo di Storia della Scienza, Florence, photograph by Scala, Florence: courtesy of the Museo del Risorgimento, photograph by Scala, Florence (2); Mary Evans Picture Library, London. **49**: FIAT Centro Storico, Turin—Archivo Storico Felici, Rome; World War II poster by Boccasile courtesy of the Museo del Risorgimento, Milan. **51**: Fresco by Pasquale Cati da Iesi, 1588, photograph by Pasquale De Antonis, Rome. **52**: Courtesy of the National Museum of the Italian Risorgimento, Turin, photograph by Fiorepress, Turin—courtesy of Biblioteca et Archivo del Risorgimento, Florence. **53**: Courtesy of Galleria Nazionale d'Arte Moderna, Rome, photograph by Pasquale De Antonis, Rome. **55**: Photo Source, London. **57**: Imperial War Museum, London. **58–65**: Romano Cagnoni, London. **66**: Barbara Gundle, Portland, Oregon. **68**: F. Gohier from Explorer/Vision International, London. **70**: Michael Boys from Susan Griggs Agency, London. **71**: Peter Carmichael from Aspect Picture Library, London. **72**: Mauro Galligani from Arnoldo Mondadori Editore, Milan. **73**: Romano Cagnoni, London. **74**: Martine Franck from Magnum, Paris. **75**: Michelangelo Durazzo from Agence A.N.A., Paris. **76**: Thomas Höpker from Bildagentur Anne Hamann, Munich. **78**: Mark Cator from Impact Photos, London. **79**: Gerd Ludwig from Visum, Hamburg. **81**: Gaetone Barone, Florence. **82**: Enrico Ferorelli from Wheeler Pictures/Colorific!, London. **83**: Thomas Höpker from Bildagentur Anne Hamann, Munich. **84–91**: Romano Cagnoni, London. **92**: Hans Wiesenhofer, Pöllau, Austria. **94**: Mauro Galligani, from Arnoldo Mondadori Editore, Milan. **96**: Joe Clarke from Robert Harding Picture Library, London; Gerd Ludwig from Visum, Hamburg. **97**: Romano Cagnoni, London. **98**: Peter Carmichael from Aspect Picture Library, London. **99**: Catherine Ashmore from Dominic Photography, London. **100**: Thomas Höpker from Bildagentur Anne Hamann, Munich. **101**: Peter Carmichael from Aspect Library, London. **102**: Romano Cagnoni, London. **103**: Firenze Academia, photograph by Scala, Florence. **105**: Romano Cagnoni, London. **106**: Michelangelo Durazzo from Agence A.N.A.,

Paris. **109**: Reproduced courtesy of the Trustees of the National Gallery, London. **110**: Courtesy of the Venezia Academia, photograph by Scala, Florence. **111**: Reproduced by courtesy of the Trustees of the National Gallery, London. **112–114**: Courtesy of Gallery Uffizi, Florence, photograph by Scala, Florence. **116**: Thomas Höpker from Bildagentur Anne Hamann, Munich. **119**: Romano Cagnoni, London. **120, 121**: David Lees, Florence. **123**: John G. Ross, Rome. **124**: Biccherna tablet courtesy of l'Archivio di Stato, Siena, photograph by Scala, Florence. **125**: Walter Rawlings from Robert Harding Picture Library, London. **126, 127**: Photograph by Chris Drake, London. (**126**: Three front lamps courtesy of Marcatré Ltd., Shaftesbury Avenue, London WC2; two rear lamps courtesy of The Lighting Workshop, Floral St., London WC2. **127**: Two centre lamps courtesy of Marcatré Ltd.; the other lamps courtesy of The Lighting Workshop.) **128**: Mario de Biasi from Arnoldo Mondadori Editore, Milan. **131**: Romano Cagnoni, London. **132, 133**: Ted Spiegel from Susan Griggs Agency, London. **134–140**: Romano Cagnoni, London. **142**: Digitized image by Creative Data, London. **143**: Marka, Milan. **145**: Romano Cagnoni, London. **147**: Map by Oxford Illustrators Ltd. **148–150**: Romano Cagnoni, London. **152**: Gianni Giansanti from Giacomino Foto, Milan. **153–155**: Romano Cagnoni, London.

BIBLIOGRAPHY

BOOKS

Acton, Harold, *The Last Bourbons of Naples*. Methuen, London, 1961.

Allum, P. A., *Italy: Republic without Government?* W. W. Norton, New York, 1974.

Allum, P. A., *Politics and Society in Postwar Naples*. Cambridge University Press, 1973.

Ardagh, John, *A Tale of Five Cities*. Secker and Warburg, London, 1979.

Arlacchi, Pino, *Mafia, Peasants and the Great Estates*. Cambridge University Press, New York, 1983.

Barzini, Luigi, *From Caesar to the Mafia*. Hamish Hamilton, London, 1971.

Barzini, Luigi, *The Italians*. Atheneum, New York, 1977.

Bethemont, Jacques, and Pelletier, Jean, *Italy: a Geographical Introduction*. Longman, New York, 1982.

Blue Guides: Blanchard, Paul, *Southern Italy*. W. W. Norton, New York, 1982.

Macadam, Alta, ed., *Sicily*. W. W. Norton, New York, 1975.

Macadam, Alta, ed., *Northern Italy*. W. W. Norton, New York, 1978.

Rossiter, Stuart, *Rome*. Benn, London, 1975.

Bull, George, *Inside the Vatican*. St. Martin's, New York, 1983.

Caesar, Michael, and Hainsworth, Peter, *Writers and Society in Contemporary Italy*. Berg, Leamington Spa, 1984.

Cairns, Christopher, *Italian Literature: the Dominant Themes*. David and Charles, Newton Abbot, 1977.

Cantacuzino, Sherban, and Brandt, Susan, *Saving Old Buildings*. Nichols Publishing, New York, 1981.

Castronno, Valerio, *L'Industria Italiana dall'ottocento a oggi*. Mondadori, Milan, 1980.

Chamberlain, Samuel, *Italian Bouquet*. Hamish Hamilton, London, 1958.

Chamberlin, E. R., and the Editors of Time-Life Books, *Rome*. Time-Life Books, Amsterdam, 1976.

Chandler, S. B., and Molinara, J. A., *The Culture of Italy*. Griffon House, Toronto, 1979.

Clark, Kenneth, *Landscape into Art*. Harper & Row, New York, 1978.

Clark, Kenneth, *Leonardo da Vinci*. Penguin Books, New York, 1976.

Clough, Shepard B., *The Economic History of Modern Italy*. Columbia University Press, New York, 1964.

Cornelisen, Ann, *Women of the Shadows*. Atlantic Monthly Press, Little Brown, Boston, 1976.

Davis, John H., and the Editors of Newsweek Book Division, *Venice*. Newsweek, New York, 1973.

Deaglio, Mario, and de Rita, Giuseppe, *Il Punto sull'Italia*. Mondadori, Milan, 1983.

de Mauro, Tullio, *Storia Linguistica dell'Italia Unita*. Editori Laterza, Bari, 1963.

Fodor's Guide to Italy. Hodder and Stoughton, London, 1983.

Gardiner, Stephen, *The Evolution of the House*. Academy Chicago, Chicago, 1980.

Gendel, Milton, ed., *An Illustrated History of Italy*. Weidenfeld and Nicolson, London, 1966.

Grant, Michael, *The World of Rome*. Sphere Books, London, 1974.

Guide to Italy. Bonechi, Florence, 1984.

Gunn, Peter, *A Concise History of Italy*. Thames and Hudson, London, 1971.

Hadas, Moses, and the Editors of Time-Life Books, *Imperial Rome*. Time-Life Books, New York, 1965.

Hale, J. R., ed., *A Concise Encyclopedia of the Italian Renaissance*. Oxford University Press, New York, 1981.

Hamilton, Olive, *The Divine Country*. André Deutsch, London, 1982.

Hearder, H., and Waley, D. P., *A Short History of Italy*. Cambridge University Press, New York, 1980.

Hobsbawm, E. J., *Primitive Rebels*. W. W. Norton, New York, 1965.

Johnson, Hugh, *Wine Companion*. Mitchell Beazley, London, 1983.

Jucker, Ninetta, *Italy*. Thames and Hudson, London, 1970.

Katz, Robert, *Days of Wrath: the Public Agony of Aldo Moro*. Granada, London, 1980.

Kelly, Francis, *Art Restoration*. David and Charles, Newton Abbot, 1971.

Kubly, Herbert, *Italy*. Sunday Times, London, 1961.

Levi, Carlo, trans. Frances Frenaye, *Christ Stopped at Eboli*. Farrar, Straus & Giroux, New York, 1947.

Lowe, Alfonso, *La Serenissima*. Cassell, London, 1974.

Lutz, Vera, *Italy: A Study in Economic Development*. Greenwood Press, Westport, Conn., 1975.

Mack Smith, Denis, *Garibaldi*. Hutchinson, London, 1957.

Mack Smith, Denis, *Italy*. University of Michigan, 1969.

Mack Smith, Denis, *Mussolini*. Weidenfeld and Nicolson, London, 1981.

Malaparte, Curzio, *Maledetti Toscani*. Vallecchi, Florence, 1976.

Marinetti, Filippo, trans. R. N. Flint and A. A. Coppotelli, *Selected Writings*. Farrar, Straus & Giroux, New York, 1972.

Martinelli, Roberto, and Padellaro, Antonio, *Il Delitto Moro*. Rizzoli, Milan, 1979.

Masson, Georgina, *The Companion Guide to Rome*, Prentice-Hall, Englewood Cliffs, N.J., 1974.

Menen, Aubrey, and the Editors of Time-Life Books, *Venice*. Time-Life Books, Amsterdam, 1976.

Michelin Tourist Guide, *Italy*. Paris, 1983.

Morris, James, *Venice*. Faber and Faber, London, 1960.

Morton, H. V., *A Traveller in Rome*. Methuen, London, 1966.

Nichols, Peter, *Italia, Italia*. Macmillan, London, 1973.

Norwich, John Julius, ed., *The Italian World*. Thames and Hudson, London, 1983.

Procacci, Giuliano, *History of the Italian People*. Weidenfeld and Nicolson, London, 1970.

Pucci, Eugenio, *The Vatican City*. International Pubns. Services, New York, 1971.

Pulgram, Ernst, *The Tongues of Italy*. Greenwood Press, Westport, Conn., 1958.

Ridley, Jasper, *Garibaldi*. Constable, London, 1974.

Romano, Sergio, *Italie*. Editions du Seuil, Paris, 1979.

Sand, Maurice, *Masques et Bouffons*. Michel et Lezy Frères, Paris, 1860.

Scalfari, Eugenio, and Turani, Giuseppe, *Razza Padrona: Storia della Borghesia di Stato*. Feltrinelli, Milan, 1975.

Shipman, David, *The Great Movie Stars: The International Years*. Hill & Wang, New York, 1981.

Silone, Ignazio, *Fontamara*. New American Library, New York, 1981.

Starr, Chester G., *The Ancient Romans*. Oxford University Press, New York, N.Y., 1971.

Stendhal, trans. Robert Sage, *The Private Diaries*. Victor Gollancz, London, 1955.

Stendhal, trans. Richard N. Coe, *Rome, Naples and Florence*. French & European Pubns., New York, 1959.

Stendhal, ed. Henri Martineau, *Vie de Rossini*. Le Divan Press, Paris, 1929.

Tisdall, Caroline, and Bozzono, Angelo, *Futurism*. Oxford University Press, New York, 1978.

Trease, Geoffrey, *The Italian Story*. Vanguard Press, New York, N.Y., 1964.

von Heintze, Helga, *Roman Art*. Weidenfeld and Nicolson, London, 1972.

Wallace, Robert, and the Editors of Time-Life Books, *The World of Leonardo*. Silver Burdett, Morristown, N.J., 1966.

Willey, David, *Italians*. BBC Publications, London, 1984.

Wiskemann, Elizabeth, *Italy since 1945*. St. Martin's, New York, 1972.

PERIODICALS

Arlacchi, Pino, "L'etica mafiosa e lo spirito del Capitalismo." *Le Scienze*, June 1984.

"Bologna Commune." *Modulo*, October/November 1978.

Economist:
  "Italian Economy Survey." May 23, 1981.
  "Eppur si Muove; a Survey of Italy." July 23, 1983.
  "Nirvana by Numbers." December 24, 1983.

Ellis, William S., "Surviving Italian Style." *National Geographic*, February 1984.

Financial Times:
  "Italian Engineering." July 16, 1984.
  "Survey: Italy." December 20, 1983.

Fox, Robert, "An Italian Romance." *Listener*, April 14, 1983.
  "Beyond Eboli." *Listener*, April 21, 1983.
  "Marsala, Missiles and Mafia." *Listener*, April 28, 1983.

Gore, Rick, "The Mediterranean." *National Geographic*, December 1982.
  "A Prayer for Pozzuoli." *National Geographic*, May 1984.

Hall, Stephen S., "Puppets and Passion." *Geo*, April 1984.

Hamblin, Dora Jane, "The Luthier's Art." *Smithsonian*, October 1983.

Newman, Cathy, "Carrara Marble." *National Geographic*, July 1982.

Panorama:
  "Droga: guerra ai merchanti della morte." April 23, 1984.
  "Quanto pesa l'elefante." March 5, 1984.

Time:
  "The Entrepreneurs of Prato." August 17, 1981.
  "Furor over Fiddles in Cremona." April 10, 1984.

The Times:
  "Italian Regions." June 16, 1983.
  "Special Report: Italy." November 4, 1983.
  "Special Report: Italy." October 31, 1984.

Warner, Marina, "The Palio." *Connoisseur*, June 1984.

INDEX

LIECHTENSTEIN

SWITZERLAND

TRENTINO-
ALTO ADIGE

• Bolzano

Trento •

LOMBARDY

VENETO

FRANCE

Aosta

VALLE D'AOSTA

Magenta   Solferino

• **Milan**

• Lodi

Cremona

Vicenza •   Padua •
Verona •

Po

M

Ivrea •   Vercelli

• Mantua

Turin •

Piacenza

• Parma   Ferrara •

PIEDMONT

• Modena

Bologna •

• Alba

EMILIA-ROMAGNA

LIGURIA

• **Genoa**

• La Spezia

• Carrara
Pietrasanta

GULF OF
GENOA

Forte dei
Marmi

• Lucca

• Prato

• Pisa   Arno   **Florence**

LIGURIAN SEA

Livorno •   TUSCANY Arezzo •
S. Gimignano •

Cor

• Siena

Per

Larderello •

Orv

ELBA

MONTECHRISTO

V

GIGLIO

Ta

SPAIN

CORSICA

TY

STRAITS OF   BONIFACIO

• Sassari

FRANCE

Nuoro •

BALEARIC ISLANDS

SARDINIA

Cagliari

M E D I T E R R A N E A N   S E A